Jim & Shirley,

Thought you might like to read this —

Thanks for all your support.

Love,
Linda

Waltzing with Katrina

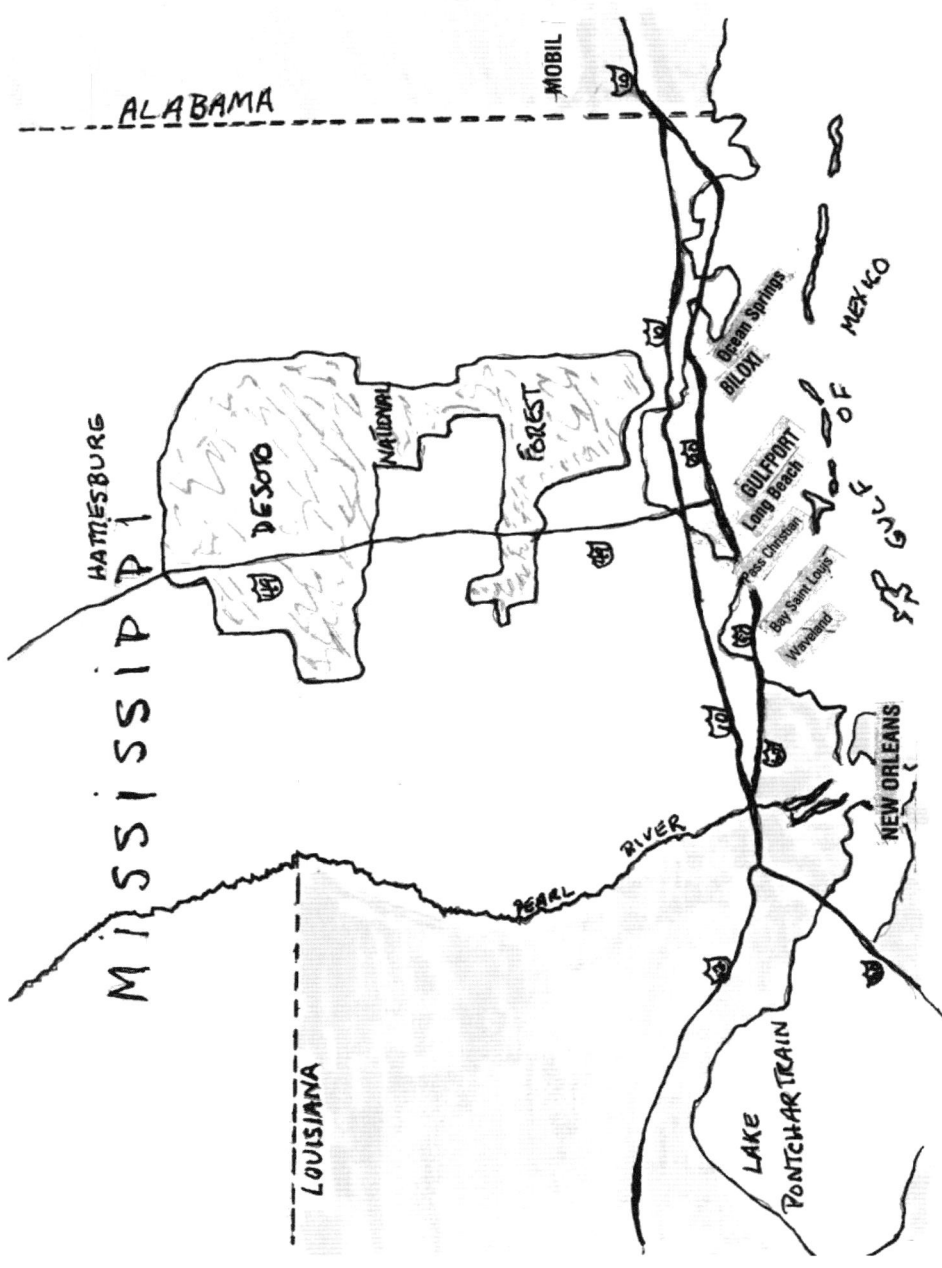

Waltzing with Katrina:

courageous stories from the people who stayed

Ann Scelba, Ph. D.

© Copyright 2006
by Ann Scelba

All rights reserved. No part of this book may be reproduced in any form or by any means, electronic or mechanical, including photocopying, recording, or any information storage and retrieval system, without permission in writing from the author.

Cover photo sunset November 2005 Pass Christian

For information:

call: 228-365-8814
or e-mail:ascelba@bellsouth.net

FIRST EDITION

Printed in the United States of America

ISBN-0-9785496-0-0

Printed on acid-free paper

To the story tellers, I honor your journey

Acknowledgments

I thank Muska Mosston from Rutgers University who helped me think outside the box. His creativity and caring helped inspire me. He taught so many about *inclusion*. Alice Glazer and Marlese Dodd supported me unconditionally and taught me critical thinking during our many years we worked together. This was during a time I was getting my wings. Jean Sadenwater's leadership taught me to trust what I know.

I gratefully acknowledge Jean Houston for pushing me past my edges during the five years in Mystery School. I am grateful to those participants who saw me as a writer and encouraged me to publish. I thank the following mystery school buddies: Dixie Crownover, for her insights and constant encouragement; Boddy Mae Matthews and Coleen Reeves, for their acceptance and inspiration; Carol Lindsey, who taught me how to get in touch with my inner knowings; Emmy Devine, for helping me to remember how much I love to dance and what it means to be a free spirit; Karen Brown (along with Jean Houston), for introducing me to Buddhism; Jill Yolen, for teaching me that love knows no bounds; Mary Giuffra, for inspiring enthusiasm for life and learning; Diane Waller, who showed me how to be creative with style; Joy Jinks, who encouraged me to see how passion in the arts and seeking truth can be combined; and Phyllis Lehman, for her friendship and showing me how to combine art, teaching, spirituality and healing.

Many friends on the Coast have encouraged me over the years and I wish to especially thank Lynn Holland, Holly Hayden, Dee Millares, Laureli Latimer, Adrienne Hemphill, Muriel Shannon, Soury, Robert Wedekind, David Reynolds, Coco Cabat, Andy McCaffrey, Betty Sue O'Brien and Lynda Baker who enthusiastically support me and this book.

I gratefully acknowledge the community of the Nourishing Place with its loving atmosphere, created by the leadership of Jane Stanley and Gail Cotton, which helped make the writing of this book possible.

This book could not have gone to print without the many people who helped in the editing process. Besides the wide range of expertise of the editors looking at this book, there was also much love and conformation offered me about the worthiness of this project. I want to thank Phyllis Lehman for helping me see how much work was needed and for introducing me to Delores Simon, an editor from Harper and Row, whose insights and information were critical in the initial stages of writing. I think Ginni Laird for working many hours on the manuscript and offering kind words of encouragement. I thank Betty Sue O'Brien for her keen eye that helped to refine this book. And Teresa Williams for spending many hours editing and providing feedback on the emotional impact of the stories. Thanks to Marianne Burkholder for the editing of the muses. Thanks to Karen Durr for giving another set of eyes to the manuscript at a critical time. Susan Traill deserves thanks for lending her keen sense of color and placement to help me make adjustments on the photos. And thanks to Terry Pollard for his technical support and superb editing to get the manuscript ready for the printer.

I have been inspired over the years by many writers. For this book I was especially helped by Pema Chodron, Thich Nhat Hanh, Paramahansa Yoganda and Rumi.

My family offered me support after the storm. I am very grateful for their love and encouragement. Thank you, Jo Crews, Jim Scelba, Joan Marks, Mary Scelba Ho, Mercedes Scelba Shorte, Victor Scelba, Nancy Kimble and Brian Marks.

The community of spirit of the four healers I work with have created a vortex of energy where anything is possible. Because of our synergy I have been able to grow in many new ways. We are soul buddies who work on multidimensional levels. This book is a physical manifestation of one part of the work I am doing with this group. In my healing process this book is born. THANK YOU! Marianne Burkholder, Regina Catalano, Gloria Murphy and Susan Traill.

Speaking of Spirit, I acknowledge and stand in awe of the help I have received from the on-physical realm who have assisted me over the years and with this book. They are the dolphins and whales, the muses, my many spirit guides, the Divine Mother, the Tibetans, the Holy Spirit, Jesus, Buddha and of course All Mighty God.

Contents

Introduction
Who's Katrina-Lisa Segarra - 1
Liberation from Self Imposed Prison-Rochelle Roberson - 11
Get some Yonder-Way-Barry Smith - 19
FEMA Man-Arman Codianne - 27
A Silent Killer-Angie, Paula, and Matt - 35
I Like Change-Deborah Lee Emery - 49
Getting out of Dodge Next Time-Cathy Brugger - 53
It went from Bad to Unbelievable-Diane Brugger - 57
Second Row Seating-Gwendolyn Canon - 63
It's Like an Opposite Life- Tu Phan - 73
The Howling and Roar of the Wind-Marianne Burkholder
 and Regina Catalano - 83
Little Things were a Big Triumph-John McManus - 93
Safe Harbor in the Storm-Jayson Sutkus and Leslie Wilder - 101
Understanding What Drives People to Extremes-Carroll Campbell - 109
Hurricane Tales-anonymous - 117
Feeling a Sense of Healing-Brian Murphy - 121
A Lot More Respect for Mother Nature-Ben Richard - 129
Getting Rid of Clutter-Rev. Jane Stanley - 133
Interesting Story-Garry McLain - 141
Lord, Look at my House-Mary Reynolds - 149
Everyone is Different-David Reynolds and Robert Wedekind - 153
I Feel Blessed- Melba Venison - 159
Epilogue - 165

Recording the following stories I asked the story tellers three questions:
1) Why did you stay during the storm?
2) How did you feel and what was your experience of the storm?
3) What did you learn from the storm and how are you different?

Introduction

"Nothing real can be threatened
Nothing unreal exits
Herein lies the peace of God"

The Course in Miracles

I began living on the Mississippi Gulf Coast in April 1993. I moved from New Jersey after retiring from teaching in public schools. The first thing I noticed here in Mississippi is that people track hurricanes. People post tracking maps on their refrigerator, publish maps in the local papers and discuss their movement on the nightly news. Maps were in many stores where I shopped. What was even more surprising was that this tracking started in late May. As a former resident of the northeast, I was amazed at the thought of mentioning a hurricane before September. I thought hurricanes developed in late August. Little did I know!

My neighbors and friends not only tracked the hurricanes, they knew all about them: longitude and latitude, feeder bands, barometric pressure, wind velocity, tornadoes and water spouts. I was learning a whole new vocabulary about the weather, and along with the vocabulary I learned of the hurricane's history here. People in the south knew their storms, how they developed, where they landed, and what the predictions were before the storm. They knew how long they lasted, the damage they did and where they were during storms of years past.

This background is to inform you, the reader, that the people on the Mississippi Gulf Coast are very knowledgeable about hurricanes and take them very seriously. With this in mind I include here several stories of courageous people and how their lives have changed forever because of a storm called Katrina. There is a bigger picture concerning this storm, and I hope to relay it here: in the telling of stories, the changed lives, as well as what we are learning about disasters and disaster relief.

According to Pema Chödrön, "shenpa" is the charge behind an emotion or thought. It has a hooked quality. It is our inability to change our automatic behavior. For example, if someone says something mean to us, we react the same way we always have. Shenpa keeps us moving away from the present moment, keeps us lost in thought, continues our numbness, perpetuates our desire to get even or get revenge, caused by old patterns of craving, wanting and needing.

I will be documenting the stories of many people who stayed and witnessed this catastrophic disaster and how they faced their "shenpa" and were willing to release it.

I believe many of these stories will show how during the storm many people had unobstructed clarity in the moment. Some learned to be very present. A greater capacity to listen to others and self seems to have emerged along with an attitude of non attachment to material things. Almost all of the stories tell of an extraordinary peace that was felt while the howling wind kept up for over 10 hours.

What the World Needs Now

*If we could read the
secret history of our enemies
we would find in each person's
story enough suffering and sorrow there
to disarm all hostilities*
                              --Longfellow

When I returned to the coast after the hurricane and went to visit my neighborhood and see my "slab"(cement foundation without structure) everyone's possessions were mixed with everyone else's. There wasn't any way to separate us; it was a lesson in our oneness, how we are all connected The funniest thing was my grandmother's sewing machine: it had moved from my building to the building behind me. I found it there beside another sewing machine. Maybe even objects crave oneness.

Katrina (which means "cleansing through torture" according to Ms. Barry, principal of Pass Christian Elementary School) seems to have awakened the Bodhichitta in many. In Pema Chödrön's book *No Time To Lose* she talks about Bodhichitta as *"the basic human wisdom that can drive away the sorrows of the world."* The word "Bodhi" means "awake," free from an ordinary confused mind, free from the illusion that we're separate from one another. "Chitta" means "heart" or "mind." Thus Bodhichitta is an awakened heart. According to Shantideva and the Buddha before him, the unbiased mind and good heart of bodhi hold the key to happiness and peace.

This has been most evident in all of the relief workers who have come to the Mississippi Gulf Coast to help us rebuild. The first ones I met were the Campus Crusade for Christ from Ohio. They drove all night to come and help for a long weekend. They slept on pew benches and many never got a shower. Eleven of them cleaned out my friend's house of wet, muddy, moldy things and respectfully saved everything they could. The next day the group swelled to 40 and was sent to several sites. What I observed most was their cooperative efforts at problem solving, i.e., how to get a refrigerator moved and on the curb. They dropped it twice and some things spilled out. The rest of the group just kept cheering them on until they succeeded, even though it was the foulest thing one could ever smell. This was carried by four guys out a back porch window, around to the front and onto the curb. Some of that same group, along with others, worked and cut a path to a house that was obstructed by a debris pile. They succeeded in moving things out so the owner could decide what to keep. During all of this moving and hauling and cutting there was never a single disagreement as to how to do something; they seemed to have left their egos behind. What an honor to see enlightened 20 year olds!

Another relief story is my regular stops to the Salvation Army truck on Menge Avenue in the Pass to pick up a chocolate bar. On one occasion the woman in front of me was feeling very sad and the man in that truck just sang her the sweetest song and it made her day and mine. There is such sweetness in us if we are not afraid to show it. Katrina has opened us up like never before, and we will never be the same.

Ann Scelba, January 19, 2006

Waltzing with Katrina

"Who's Katrina?"

Lisa Segarra and her husband Jay have lived on the beautiful waterfront of Ocean Springs, Mississippi since April Fools Day 2000. Natives of Boston, they had lived in Ocean Springs since Jay, an Air Force doctor, was stationed at Keesler Air Force Base in 1987.

We were in New Orleans the week before the storm. It was a great time eating, drinking, playing, and celebrating a friend's 60th birthday. We went home to our French Quarter Apartment where we woke up to banging and hammering sounds on Royal Street. There were loud nailing noises outside our shuttered French quarter studio apartment's doors. We dressed and went out for coffee. We noticed people were closing up shutters and store fronts writing "Katrina, go away." I asked Jay, "Who's Katrina?" We walked along Royal Street and some stores were opened; I bought a gift from a perfumery-saw more boarding up. We were asked if we were going home, went into a bar and saw coverage on the hurricane and still didn't think it would come to Mississippi. It looked like Texas. However, people in New Orleans were certain it was coming to them. My daughter Katherine called from California, where she was visiting an old roommate from Brown, and asked if we would get her cats from Soniat Street in New Orleans and bring them home to Mississippi, as her roommates were evacuating. So we left with 2 cats in a cat carrier and drove from New Orleans to Mississippi late Saturday afternoon. It was surreal. We passed a police barricade keeping people out of Mississippi. We were one of the last cars through the police road block on Interstate 10 heading east about 3:00 p.m. Saturday afternoon.

I spent Sunday boarding up and bringing kayaks, life preservers, dishes, wine glasses, and a small refrigerator from the pier. I moved the lawn chairs and did the rest of the general hurricane preparation. I didn't really board up; I said that because I usually do, but I didn't have the time. My plan was to put trucks in front of the house as a wind sheer, using the Suburban, so I moved everything and put trucks there instead of boarding up. As an afterthought we moved the Mercedes up to our office on Government Street. My secretary Cora was preparing the office. She brought plants in and drew the blinds. We came back, and I made a big pot of vegetable stew and I also made lasagna. We weren't sure what we were going to do. Maybe go to the Gulf Hills Country Club where everyone went the last time to have a party. But my friend Becky Feder called and said, "You gotta get out of there! You're coming to my house, that's it!" So after cleaning my house, doing laundry from the weekend (that's what you do when you don't think anything is going to happen), we went to Becky Feder's house with bottles of wine, lasagna, and a bag of clothes. I didn't take jewelry or cats. Becky is bigger than life itself and had the thermostat down to 60 degrees in case the AC went out. After spending 3 hours in a meat locker and going outside to pretend to smoke when I really went to warm up, Jay said, "Lisa, we better go home to get the cats. The TV says we are going to have a 22 foot storm surge." I thought they were hyping it up and getting everyone upset and in turmoil. I thought: I am going home and going to bed. I'm tired of this and freezing. On Monday, at 12:30 a.m. we went home. I fed the cats, who were anxious, and went to bed. I dragged a suitcase full of clothes to the middle of the floor and went to bed and was sick of the whole thing. I've been preparing for this for two days and I'm done.

I slept soundly from 1:00 a.m. to 6:30 a.m. with three cats on top of me. The other cat, Kate had said, only attacks men and will claw and bite if provoked. That one was hiding in Katherine's room. I did wake up during the night to loud winds and trees falling on the roof but went back to sleep. The roof is monolithic cement. I never worried about trees on it. Jay didn't sleep a wink. He was up pacing and watched the news on the internet. Ocean Springs had shut off the water to the house sometime before we returned from Becky's house. So when I woke up I had to go down into the rising water to get water to flush the toilets. It was wild out there. The pier was no longer visible. The water was half-way up the driveway and the wind was howling. I noticed that my kayak cribs had floated away and the kayaks were hung up on the wire fence. By then I had put on a one piece red gortex sailing suit, red wellies and red life preserver. I put Jay in his blue one, offered him wellies, then I went out and moved the kayaks and tied them to the tree that was closer to the house. The water was rising, so I got on the Hobie Cat and rode it a bit, getting whipped about. And Jay said, "Stop playing. This is no time to play, get in the house." I remember looking out and the street was completely flooded with 13 feet of water. "There was no way out. I was thinking. Why not play, what else can I do?" I went and got more buckets of water; I appeared serious and productive. There was just so much energy, more than anything I had ever seen in a long time. I'd been in northeasters with more wind and sailed in races with more wind, taken on 3 or 4 people for more ballast.

Jay was meanwhile putting a ladder behind the house that could lead up to the flat roof. He told me to get the cat carriers just in case, but we both weren't sure we'd need them. And the water was still coming, slowly coming but the wind had died down. And I thought is that all, much to do about nothing? I went back in and tried to figure out how to make coffee. The electricity was down at that point. I noticed water was beginning to slowly rise again and the wind was picking up, so I got everything from the floor up onto the bed and dressers and thought about taking my jewelry, silver and photos of mother, father and family with me, but where to? So I put them up high on a back shelf and put my jewelry up on an armoire and put it up in the highest spot and raced through the house putting everything on the ground up. And then I noticed water was on the patio, winds were picking up, more howling, and water began to seep into the cracks of the sliding glass doors. I raced to get Jay to tell him water was coming in. I got my cats and left 2 others for him. I left Bling-Bling and attack cat for Jay. As I was coming back through the front of the house, the wind knocked in the glass front doors and then a huge wave just rolled right in. I grabbed the cats, (now in cat carriers) and took them out the back door, up the ladder to the roof. Jay was close behind with attack cat and Bling-Bling in tow.

There was no time in the end for jewelry, photos or other things. I even left my nap sack by the side door. I did go back in for my purse (through the water up to my knees and thighs with wellies), waded in the kitchen, grabbed the nap sack and up the ladder I went. We did think to bring a rope and water with us. We got up and pulled the ladder up behind us; the winds were very strong. We were clever enough to situate ourselves and the cats behind the sky light that acted as a wind sheer and just sat there for a while. The water was now all the way through our house, and the waves were cresting on our patio.

I had to get up and look around. I watched the water rising over my neighbors to the left front steps and watched a tornado rip off their roof and throw it into the back yard flying past me on the roof. With another gust of wind and low roar came what must have been another tornado, never touching the water. It picked up Edsel Ruddim's roof, to our right, and then dropped it about 2 feet from where it had been. I had to duck because the wind over my head was so strong. At that point the water hadn't entered their house yet and had only a few feet into mine. They were on pilings up about 22 feet; we're at 18 feet above sea level.

After we saw other people's roofs come off and the waves started coming through our house, I noticed my red suitcases that I took to Becky's were now floating past up out through my living room doors and my makeup in a gold lama satchel was floating past me in the debris. I said, "My God, Jay, I need my red lip stick if I'm in a hurricane I need my red lips." And Jay threw down the ladder as I held the top in place and caught my makeup bag as it floated by. Not long afterwards my father in-law's cello that he played in the Paris Symphony came floating by in its case. Jay jumped in the hallowing waters and retrieved it and passed it up to me. Just as my cello he brought me 3 years ago for Christmas in its green case came by, and he got that, too. Then he came back up the ladder. He wasn't up long before he started thinking of other things he was missing and he thought about his wallet, our passports and Padi dive cards in his study. He decided to descend the ladder one more time to the water over our heads, into the flooded house to retrieve them. There was no talking him out of it. He was down the ladder before I could say "don't." And as he swam to the door with his life vest on he said, "Stand on the ladder to hold it still because it is floating away." I had to put my full weight and press on the roof to keep the ladder from going and taking me with it. My arms were getting tired, and I was getting worried about Jay who had gone into what was left of my studio; I couldn't see in. The waves were too high, and our baby grand piano was lunging fiercely back and forth with the waves. That was the only time I was frightened, and it was for Jay. I had to calm myself down. I couldn't see Jay, and I could see into my son's bedroom and it was chaos in there. I had to decide to abandon the ladder and go in after him or to hang on and wait, so we both had a way to get back up on the roof. And just as I was ready to battle the piano and go in after him, he emerged over the piano top and swam out. He didn't have his wallet.

I kept saying "this is surreal," while within moments the waves crashed through our house, and I noticed a large square top floating past us and said, "Jay there's a hot tub, oh wait, that's our hot tub," and it floated surrealistically past our house and turned the corner into the backyard. The waves were now crazy, cresting in the front yard as well as back. Water was coming from the Bayou behind us and from the sea. It was for all the world like being in the Atlantic Ocean on a cruise ship, and you can't land at any port so wicked wild it was out there. About this point I felt this is so violent and wild I started to pray for my neighbors, and I was glad I had a flat roof and hadn't changed it. I had thought it was always so ugly. I prayed to the Blessed Mother to calm the seas.

I have a statue of the Blessed Mother by the pier, and I moved her higher and higher as I moved the boats. At some point I told her. "You've got to swim, Mary." She was too heavy to come on the roof. I know she has a sense of humor. I became like a beacon of white light trying to calm the sea. I would look out and the sea was a brown fury of waves. The telephone poles were under water and no longer visible. You could hear the low howling of tornadoes. I had to duck and had water below me and tornadoes above me.

After reapplying my red lip stick (which is what I do when I get nervous in an attempt to calm myself and feel normal), I told Jay who was now exhausted, who had not slept and was forlorn about having lost his wallet, that it was okay, that as long as he was holding on to both cat carriers he could rest his head against the sky light and go to sleep. I told him I would wake him if anything bad happens. Within minutes he was sound asleep, and I could hear his snoring even over the sounds of the storm. This was my chance to explore. If I timed my climb onto the higher roof to avoid the swaying oak branches I could get up there and look down the sky lights. I saw my bedroom that was nothing but a sea of mud, then into my daughter's bedroom where her bed was spinning. It was like looking into a front loaded washing machine and watching everything spin around.

If I timed the waves properly I could lie flat on the roof and hang over the overhang and look into my dining room and watch the waters violently flow through. My trucks were banging against the columns below me, and I prayed again that the Lord wouldn't let the house come down because I needed those columns to stay. I really did. I prayed again for God to calm things down, calm the sea down, and for the safety of my friends and towns people who I was really worried about. By now, I was now praying for the whole Gulf Coast and their safety. Somehow I felt completely safe and was enveloped by a calm even in the middle of this violent storm. I was never worried. I remember telling Jay that I was awfully glad I was on the roof with him and not someone else.

We went up on the roof about 7:45 a.m. and it wasn't until about 2:30 p.m. that the water slowly receded. We weren't able to get off the roof until 4:00 p.m. We put the ladder down when the water was still knee high, and I sloshed about in what was complete and utter devastation. My first thought was what a mess; how am I ever going to clean this up! The entry into the house was blocked with pier pilings, rubble, boards from other homes, so I couldn't get into my house, and nothing was where it was suppose to be. To any organized soul, that's a very bad thing!

We waited until the water was nearly gone from the back of the house so we could rest the cats out of the wind on the ground. We were both sort of wandering around in disbelief when I heard a four wheeler race by heading toward my neighbor's house. I tried to run after it, but the winds were stronger on the ground than they had been on the roof, and it took me a long time to get the short distance between the houses. I kept yelling into the wind, "Is everybody all right. Do you need a doctor?" I didn't think anyone had stayed, but I was worried now that my elderly neighbor who lived in the house where I saw the roof fly off, might have stayed. And I kept yelling and the man had stopped in front of the neighbor's old kitchen door, I say "old" because the kitchen wasn't there anymore. Amazingly four young men came piling out of the vehicle, their eyes round with awe! Finally I caught up with them and shouted, "Does anyone need a doctor?" Later the man in the four wheeler thought I was Aqua-woman from a helicopter sent to rescue him. I had red wellies, red gortex, a red life vest, and a blue bike helmet with Red Lips. The boys had been home for summer break, one from Australia, one from England and two from Ocean Springs. They were 19-20 years old. All of them had just finished a survival course and thought it would be fun to weather out this storm. They were actually washed out of their home and into a tree where they had spent the same hours I spent on the roof. I couldn't see them because of the trees between us. Although unharmed, they were actually dazed as nothing in that survival course had taught them about this.

It was this group that led Jay and I out. This was the only route out because so many trees and houses had blocked so many roads off East Beach. Somehow San Souci St. was open, and Jay and I traipsed out of there in our life vests carrying the cat carriers and hitched a ride from the chief of police to our office on Government St. There I found my amazing secretary checking the office after the storm. She cried when she saw us. She thought we were dead. I had asked the policeman about my friend Becky and her house. He said the bridge was out, and he said no one had been back there to Iola Drive. Our secretary took us home to her house and later we went next door to where my gardener lives and ended up staying for six weeks. Luckily, because of my love for the garden, I had been out there day after day tending the herbs and trees with my gardener, and we became good friends, Thank God, I didn't hire her to just dig by herself.

I guess I would simply say in the days that followed I returned to the beach, and my house was the only house left standing on the beach. I was very grateful that our lives were spared as well and very grateful for friends and family who supported us through this.

I guess I want to say, I learned how little I really needed, how few things I really needed and became more acutely aware of how God provides you with what you need and ask for.

One of the first things I found when I got to the beach was the rosary that had been on my bedpost, that room scoured and clean. The bed was gone, nothing but the rosary unscathed. The Blessed Mother had a bit of derma abrasion but was otherwise untouched and still standing. As I would recall things and dreaming about them at my gardener's house I would ask God to help me find them, and in this way I retrieved my sterling and pearls and most of the jewelry Jay has given me over the years. What matters here is not the material things, but God is bountiful and gives us what we ask for and emotionally need.

It is amazing to be here. Had I been on any other roof on the beach it would have been perilous, and I was thankful for my flat roof; I was thanking God.

I feel my inner core is stronger because of this. I feel I am able to do more things, what used to be obstacles, I can do now.

Musings

How often do we deny things that are right in our face? Sometimes it takes a Mac truck to get it in our heads that something big is happening. Observing with curiosity and awe are the steps along the path towards acceptance and this opens our channels to spirit. Sometimes it takes the awareness of a very serious situation or a frightening experience to then turn to prayer or guidance. Sometimes it's those moments that bring clarity. Often we forget to be present and dissociate because it is just too scary. Our psyche is only able to take in and hold so much. Our ability in normal circumstances to confront stress determines what we can do in times of great emotional trauma. Our nervous system is a living growing organism. Traumas can inhibit growth; the maturation of the nervous system is impinged upon in ways we do not fully understand. Katrina taxed everyone's nervous system beyond capacity. There is too much devastation for our minds, bodies, psyche, spirits to comprehend. In the grieving process, we can go through steps and come out on the other side healed. Grieving with Katrina is constantly being re-traumatized by the endless scenery of rubble and debris, the constant frustration of dealing with insurance companies and FEMA and the inefficiency of all forms of local, state and federal agencies. On top of this there is the loss of friends, community, property and a way of life. How do we get beyond this? In the following chapters we may glean some insight into a unique healing process that is derived from the greatest catastrophe to hit the United States. Katrina may turn out to be the greatest gift that we have ever received.

"Liberation from Self Imposed Prison"

Rochelle Roberson lives in Biloxi, Mississippi and is a manager for Blockbuster Video.

I stayed for two reasons, says Rochelle Roberson of Biloxi. Technically, I didn't have time to leave by the time I left work; I'm an assistant store manager for Blockbuster, and I felt obligated to stay and work. I spent all day Sunday boarding up windows; I felt there was a reason to really board up this time, a sixth sense. I listened to my inner voice. This is the end of the first year that I really am listening to my inner guidance. Other hurricanes I only boarded up a few windows with plywood and nails. This time I asked my neighbor to tightly secure all windows with screws. The time to travel was too tight by the time I got the windows done. There was no clear destination as to where to go.

My car is a city car, not a highway car. I found a friend to stay with in Gulfport off Courthouse near Gulfport High, close to the tracks.

Before I accepted differences in people but did not allow them in me. I am freer now, accepting myself even though it is different from my family. I am a Christian. Instead of focusing on one religion, I've allowed myself to believe in the spirituality of Christianity and not just the practices.

I grew up in a family where religion was the foundation of thinking, doing, everything. My religion is the way I express my spirituality. I had choices of churches as a child (my mother is Baptist my grandma Methodist), just as long as I went to church.

I stayed because of a sense of independence. Everyone told me I had to leave. I am reveling in the notion to be grown now. I'll probably never be grown in my family's eyes. Part of asserting independence is accepting the consequences.

The fact that I was here and survived it without freaking out, I feel I am a better person because of it. I'm no longer afraid of little things. Once you go through this, little things don't scare you anymore. Day-to-day life is more stressful because of the environment, but the things that used to depress me do not because I survived it. My priorities have changed, shifted. I am more appreciative of the little things, and my level of patience has grown.

If you'd gone off on me I wouldn't retaliate; it would bother me. It no longer bothers me. If this hurricane didn't change you, nothing's going to change you. If someone is having difficulty, I can tolerate other people's frustrations more. I no longer take things personally.

Once I read the *The Four Agreements* (Miguel Ruiz), Number 3 is don't take things personally, and I took it to heart. The storm actually helped me get there easier. My life changed. I don't get angry as much anymore. I started finding my equilibrium, balance better. I was less worried what "you were doing toward me" and I just took care of me. That's a handful on its own. The storm actually helped me get closer to finding my own center.

Thursday night before the storm I went to a friend's house and allowed her to do a Tarot reading; I never allowed it before. The things that were said were right on, and I realized she had a guide and I could sense that person. I'm learning to notice when there is a presence among us. I actually listened and opened up and realized it is time for my own quest.

Sitting in a very hot, dark house for five days, I know there is a guide. I've found that I can acknowledge this and accept it and know everyone doesn't believe what I believe. I will meet people that don't have my best interest at heart and know I need to listen to my instincts. It is definitely a lesson learned. Most people that I know that have stayed have a sense of peace and confidence. I now can say what I feel; if I'm afraid, I'll say it. I now know how each one of my family will react. And I now accept it instead of fighting it. I no longer resist what I know is true. I accept it. It is such a wonderful feeling; it is a very liberating feeling. What Katrina actually did was liberate me from my self-imposed prison.

There are days I revert back to old familiar ways. Yet I still know the door is now open, and I can be out instead of in and it is a wonderful feeling.

I was at my friend's house with her and her husband, his dog and cat. Part of the time I had a huge sense of anxiety, not being able to know how everyone is. I couldn't get any phone calls out.

During the storm I remember sleeping, waking up, going back to sleep. I wasn't scared; I noticed I wasn't scared and was ecstatic about not being afraid. I noticed people sitting outside across the street; I waved to them. They were in a protected space and could not be harmed. We went outside not during the worst wind, during the eye. There is the oddest thing during a hurricane: I can breathe really well (I have asthma) and then I can hardly breathe. I can tell pressure changes. When I wasn't asleep or in the living room, I put on head phones and tried to go back to sleep. I've been hanging out with my imagination lately.

In the storm at 2:00 a.m. the lights went out, and we were prepared for the cable to go. Once the lights went out, we had candles, then talked for a while. My friend was like, "bring it on," I couldn't do that: I felt it was disrespectful because I felt Katrina was a force to be reckoned with. I recognize that I chose to stay, and I was not going to thumb my nose to her. This is nature, mother nature and I'm very respectful of mother nature.

So after a while I went to bed with my CD player with very soothing music, and I allowed the night to embrace me and I went to sleep. I slept in the office with the door shut; it was a cat free space. The house had two other adults and 8 cats. I woke up to an empty living room and went to the windows and watched the wind blow for a while.

The day after the storm, Tuesday, we walked the beach; my mind snapped, it shut off, I could not process it. I had to put it away and accept the reality that THIS building is gone and that this building is gone. That is why I had to leave for a month to recover emotionally, spiritually, and mentally.

I am stronger now because I recognize that what I saw, the devastation, was more than I could bear. I felt guilty because my house survived, and I had to learn sympathy and empathy without getting caught up in the guilt.

The only negative thing of the hurricane is I stopped writing. I like to write short stories and fiction. They are a collaboration on what has happened and what I'd like to happen. I put those together and that's where I get my short stories. I like to refer to it as "fiction based on truth."

This storm allowed me to grow, and I see it as very positive; something seen as catastrophic has helped me to not back track. I'll never be able to find that level of ignorance again. Sometimes ignorance is bliss. I now realize the intangible things have just as much presence as the living things. It's no longer separate. These multiple worlds have collided. I used to live on one plane, and now I have an understanding of how multi-realities react, more than dimension or reality. If I say dimension or reality, I have a fixed idea of what it is, and I'm starting to learn it has no fixed origin.

Katrina was a very tough blessing for me at a very high cost. It was a blessing because I'm a better person from it. The high cost is the day-to-day stress it causes. I am thankful my house survived with no water, though when the adjuster came he showed me where there was damage, structural damage even though it looks good on the outside. In a sense people mirror this. They look whole but there is a lot of structural damage.

Musings

*Let us remember that
within us there is a place of
immense magnificence.*

--Teresa of Avillon

There seems to be something about the energy of the storm that can allow us the possibility to open up and awaken to a much grander being. Many of the stories I heard tell of a change of beliefs, values, or character of the people who stayed. Besides the physical changes of barometric pressure, tornadoes, and high winds, there seems to be a great emotional, mental, and spiritual shift in these story tellers. We can ask ourselves, how have we changed from watching the storm's TV coverage or hearing stories from friends or relatives?

An awakening seems to be afoot; can you feel it? Sloshing around in the washing machine of the psyche, our perception and awareness is growing. When we allow a tragedy of this magnitude to enter our being, we are forever changed. In the process we have choices. We need to be okay in whatever choices we make and know that is the best we can do at the time. We may stretch our knowing, our behaviors, and our habits until we are not sure we are the same person; we are much more. Along with this change it is important we are open to our own state and to be truly compassionate about where we are and how we are in all situations. If we can observe ourselves and be okay with whatever we see, we will have that same ability to see others okay in their struggles. Compassion starts at home before we can have it for others. This is truly a time for self compassion.

One thing that seems to be happening is the visceral acceptance of the oneness of all things. On the physical level we received a great picture of this when everyone's things were mixed up with everyone else's. It was impossible to tell what belonged to whom. We were in the pot together and stirred frantically until we got the message. There are no boundaries among any of us; we are all made up of the same stuff. The only thing that separates us is our own stubbornness to refuse to see the obvious.

Katrina didn't discriminate by wealth, skin color, nationality, profession, job status, age, mental ability, physical ability, gender, sexual orientation, religious belief, or any other way we separate ourselves from one another. She hit us all, whether it was about our things, our loved ones, our environment, or our false stability. Everyone got it on some deep level. What we do with it is up to each of us. There are incredible possibilities in front of us if we are open, present, and awake.

Blue heron using debris for lookout

Mercedes steering wheel signaling peace!

"Get some Yonder-Way"

Barry Smith is a police officer in Pass Christian, Mississippi. He moved from Houston, Mississippi in 1972 to the Gulf Coast. His police work began as part time in 1995, and in 1999 he became a full-time officer. He lives in Gulfport, Mississippi with his wife and children.

I have learned not to stay through a hurricane. We stayed through two before, and it was nothing. I came in at midnight. The Chief said, "You live in Gulfport, stick around here you might not get out." So I went to the backroom and relaxed for a couple of hours. The wind picked up after three to four hours, and it woke me up. It sounded like a woman whistling. I thought about my son, daughter and wife as I heard the storm, and I got up. The dispatcher said it looked like it was coming right at us. She said, it will be bad for us. We saw the TV and knew we were on the east side of it. That was not good for us. The east side of a hurricane is the worst side to be on. I could hear the wind blow through the building, and the Chief said we might have to leave to get in a higher building because of the water. Word came down from the Chief to lock the building down and go to the library. The Police station is 24 feet and the library was 27 feet above sea level. So we get up there, and the rain starts coming down. We left the station at 6:00 a.m. We had all the wind before that. We got several calls from Hispanic males: "Help, help, can't speak English! Send help!" On our rounds we had told them to leave, and they said they had nowhere to go. So I see the address on 911 and put the name with the face when I hear the dispatcher and the voice, and told them to leave the low-lying area. They couldn't understand and didn't have a way to leave.

Everyone knew Mrs. Seal, 84 years old. I finally got her convinced to leave in a car with her neighbor at 2:00 p.m. Sunday. Then at 4:45 p.m. I see her going to the neighbor's house in my rear view mirror as I am patrolling. As soon as I got to the railroad track I saw her go back to her house. The neighbor wasn't there. We found Mrs. Seal the next day.

Only two of the houses I went to to ask them to leave, didn't. Maybe I should be more forceful. I went to a house with another officer; his brother tried to get him out. I knew him from before. After 20-30 minutes he said, "It's my time to go and I'm not going to leave." His sister came, and we said we'd be back in 30 minutes and arrest him. He said, "So take me." Then I got reassigned and found out later he had drowned. They found him at Timberidge; he had been at Henderson, about a mile away. He rode out the storm in a trailer, and the storm washed it away.

We were in the Library and started relaxing; I took my gun belt off and kept saying "it's getting rough out here." There were eleven male officers, one dispatcher and one female warrant officer. The Chief said, "It didn't get that high during Camille." We sat around relaxing and joking. The older officers reading books and newspapers, the younger ones taking pictures. You could hear the wind; the sound was distinct like tornadoes. Then we looked out the window and saw a row of plastic cups with BP on them, and we said BP (gas station) must have taken a beating. The rain started getting up and then slowed down again. We tried to secure everything we could. We moved the cars back toward City Hall; then we noticed the water started standing. About 10:00 -10:30 a.m. I noticed the water in the parking lot was flowing. At 11:00 it was coming down Heirn Avenue, coming down the top of the hill. It started raining hard. Then the water started standing at the door. The Chief said, "It doesn't look too good; it didn't get that high during Camille." The library was built after hurricane Camille 30 years ago.

The water was halfway up the tires in the parking lot. During the moving of the cars one of the guys looked at the beach and said, "The water on highway 90 is over the beach". The Chief didn't believe it. We started seeing water knee deep in the parking lot and got worried. At 11:00-11:30 we stopped reading the newspapers. Now we were looking for somewhere to go in the storm. We noticed the blue lights on the police cars were flashing; they started short circuiting. First we grabbed newspapers and put them by the door to keep from getting the carpet wet. Then we noticed the pressure was popping the screws on the door. They kept working their way out, and the water was coming through.

Chief said, "It doesn't look good." We called the sheriff's department and told them to get us out. He had no one. Patrol cars were flashing lights. The water rose halfway to the door knob. We couldn't see the ground in the parking lot. We had a big army truck--a deuce and 1/2-- on the north side of the library. It was for troop transport. We could only see the hood. Then cars started floating. "Sure doesn't look good," the Chief said. "I rode it out during Camille." The other officers said, "You rode it out during Camille in the Clerk's office building, which is now under water. Sure doesn't look good." One of the cars started floating across the parking lot and went to the west side in the woods. When the next car started moving the Chief said, "Get your stuff. That one may come through the door. I heard a bloop-like thud and looked up; we were on top of the book shelves, and the water was on the floor. The car broke the door frame and glass, and the water from the parking lot came in the library. The wave current pushed everyone to the north side of the building. The Chief said, "Better get these windows broken cause of the pressure." We couldn't move; the water was rising high and fast. We shot the glass, and the bullets started ricocheting and no glass broke. Just as Chief told us to stop shooting after we had shot 30 rounds, and they were ricocheting, he beat on the door with a chair and it broke the lock on the door. It sounded like a train; the waves sucked him out the door. It was only a 2 foot wide opening. The carpet on the floor was grabbing our legs and kept us unbalanced; our feet got tangled in the carpet, and we were tripping over each other and the carpet.

I could hear shouting, "Get to the door, get to the door!" Over there it sounded like a train. Everyone was pushed to the door by the current and pinned up against the wall. We tried to work our way out, three at the door, five or six behind and we looked up to see what was holding us back; it was the carpet. The Chief grabbed the first two coming out and a wave got them and pushed them through. They were all circled around the column with the overhead canopy, six-eight holding on. The last four-five were holding onto a TV cable wire. It was like a scene from a science fiction movie, and all of a sudden the screws are coming loose from the cable wire. For 30 minutes they were holding onto the wire; the water was coming in waves through the door. Sergeant said, "We got to get to higher ground." He got loose from the group and got to the northwest side of the library and got on the roof. So the Chief said, "Everyone get to the roof;" it was still raining and the waves are coming. We got everyone up there; I waited till last, I'm 300 plus pounds. I said "I'll stay down here." The Chief said, "No you got to go up." I get a cramp on the way up, so they're pulling and pushing. The chief is pushing. I'm on the roof, and they don't know what is wrong. I said, "I think I'm going crazy." I'm yelling "cramp, cramp." It seems the cramp lasted longer than the storm. I'm telling them to punch my leg and the Chief said," Get him on his feet." So I get up there riding it out on the roof and as soon as the water comes up, all we can see is a few inches of the army truck. We can't see the Clerk's office. It is just a pool of water.

We stay up there about an hour. I saw a boat flopping up in the water. Someone says, "Maybe I can swim to the boat." The Chief said, "No, wait till the water goes down." When the water went down we saw the boat was attached to a truck. After that we rode it out till the water went away. We check the damage in the library. Trees were down, wires were down. We knew the department was gone; we saw the 2nd floor of the church. The first floor was missing. We stayed about 3 hours. We went to St. Paul's church about dusk. Then two investigators and another officer from DeLisle came. They had to cut their way into the city. They couldn't get in at first; they went back to get a chainsaw.

The sheriff had told them our last known position in the library on Scenic Drive. At 10:30 p.m. they found us in St. Paul's. All 13 made it. One time I was trying to push the dispatcher to the roof and a wave went over my head two times. They knew I "needed to get some yonder-way." I couldn't swim; I swim like a brick.

I got a ride to Gulfport from an officer in Long Beach. He gave three of us a way home. My wife was outside most of the time. She said it was like a light show. The worst part of the deal was not knowing where my family was. I kept hearing that south of the tracks got demolished and washed away.

I think when they say Category 5, Leave. When they say direct hit, Leave. Personally, when they say hurricane, Leave. It was mandatory we stay. The next storm it will be an option. We understood we would get fired; officers got suspended for not returning in a timely manner.

The worst deal is the two people I tried to save. I still see them in my face, and I'll never forget them. I think that the storm brought everyone closer together. There was competition before the storm. This shift did this. Now it's WE did this.

We lost 16 out of 24 guns. I found my gun 45 days after the storm. I was worried that we had lost four to six guns after the storm because we couldn't grab them as we were getting out the door. The AmeriCorp kids found them.

Everyone learned something from this storm. The first 10-12 weeks I had to go to EOC Civil Defense Building every day, 12 hours a day and had problems at my own home. I was the one everyone spoke to on the phone: "What do you need?"

I have stopped taking everything for granted. I live one day at a time now. I listen a whole lot more now to my wife. I have patience with folks.

I use to brush my kids off. Now I listen to what they say, and I'm more involved in their schools. Sure showed me not to taken anything for granted.

Musings

How do we learn patience and forgiveness? Does it take a devastating hurricane, a great loss? Maybe sometimes we need a push to get to our inner core, that place that is all good, all knowing and is gentle. Katrina washed away a lot of things. Some of what she washed away is our outer resistance shield of protection that keeps us separated from others and ourselves. This washing away is as the elementary principal Ms. Barry said, a cleansing. Not a simple cleansing but one that reaches our core. In this washing process we shed our skins and are raw and open to more possibilities and feelings. We learn to honor ourselves and in the process honor those around us. We become more cheerful, experience joy, and know the preciousness of nature and our surroundings. How many of us long to see the beach again clean and the water sparkle and the sea birds playing in the sand? As we see this return we recognize the mystery of the universe and how grateful we are for what we have. It is impossible then to take anything for granted. When you have experienced near-death, an inner truth comes forth, and we remember who we really are. This is the lesson of Katrina and all disasters if we are willing to feel and listen.

FEMA Man with friend

"FEMA Man"

Arman Codianne moved to the Mississippi Gulf Coast from California in 1981. In 1987 he moved back to California. Four years later in 1991 he was back on the coast. He moved to Waveland, Mississippi on the Gulf Coast in 1995 where he still resides. Arman is a certified massage therapist and healing touch practitioner who, before graduating from massage school, was diagnosed with multiple sclerosis. This increased his challenges as he tented on his destroyed property waiting for a FEMA trailer. He was denied a trailer initially until he went to the newspapers to tell his story. Driving around with a life-size stuffed doll with the words FEMA Man on it shows the sense of humor Codianne has. CNN has done a follow-up on Arman's story.

Before the storm I repainted the house, repaired and painted porch boards, bought all new furniture for the apartment next door and got a renter. I choose the color of the house "yellow brick road," from my favorite movie "The Wizard of OZ." I built a large garden shed two days before the hurricane. I left before the shingles were put on. I left Sunday, August 28th between 7:00 and 9:00 a.m. to go to Winnsboro, LA. with friend Mary Frost. We drove to Baton Rouge on Wednesday, after the storm. I watched on the news everything that was happening and didn't realize the devastation. On the way home, Mississippi Public Radio had callers calling in saying, "Waveland does not exist."

eyes out. Then we said, "Yes, Waveland does exist because people are alive."

In Baton Rouge, Louisiana, we stayed with one of Mary's friends for six weeks. We came back on September 14th. We came back for the cat, thinking the cat was dead. We had put the cat in the house on the washer and dryer with food. We thought we'd be gone 2-3 days. When we came back the house was gone. My neighbor Brian heard the cat meowing for food the night before outside his tent. I gave Brian a big hug when we got back.

Flashback--Saturday afternoon I heard on the radio the hurricane had 175 mile an hour winds and it was a Category 5 headed for Mississippi/Louisiana border. That made me change my mind and go.

I had seven harmonicas in the closet in a bag. I found two out of seven and they worked so I sat down and played them. My friend Mal brought me five new ones. "It was a smily point, it was a good thing". I was on the steps playing the harmonica blues, Katrina blues, and people asked me why I'm smiling. I said, "Why not?"

My neighbor Brian, a stone's throw away, stayed. I told him, he and his mother could come to Winnsboro with us. He said they got through Camille, they were staying. He took her to a safe place, supposedly, back down by Da Beach House in Bay St. Louis. The building collapsed, and she died and was found days later. They found breathing tubes in her noise so they knew it was her.

Brian had stayed in his house next door and at one point checked my house and shed, and it was okay when winds were kicking butt. The wind and water washed him out of his 2nd story house with his dog and debris. He tried to ride the wave, and he was being sucked down. He thought he was gone, then he came up. He was holding on to trees and went with the trees. He didn't hold on to anything he knew would hurt him. He ended up on a house at the tracks for two hours. After the water subsided he found his way home about 1/4 mile away. Then he walked home and was in a state of shock because everything was gone. He grew up across the street and lived in this house for 40 years. It was the only life he knew.

We were looking for our cat, and rescue workers from the Mobile, SPCA were here. We described him, and they said they had him. We could came over and get him at 6:30 p.m. We went to get him, and he was so happy to see us. He was a little skinnier. He wouldn't eat for the rescue SPCA workers, but when he saw us, he rubbed up against us and started eating. They gave us a case to take the cat to Baton Rouge.

The first couple of nights in Baton Rogue he walked all over us. The first night he stayed no more than an arm's length away.

When I was in Baton Rouge, me and some other healers went to the first responders and worked on them 6:00 - 9:00 a.m. after they came in off their shifts. Asked if I needed clothes, I replied, "I have no drawers to put my draws in." One lady the same size as I am gave me two pairs of jeans.

The house was in pieces; it must have imploded. I wondered how the cat got out when there was no way out. We just wandered through the rubble and were in awe of what happened; seeing your town gone, brick post office gone, town hall gone, no houses, the walking wounded, no diagram of how to act, everyone in shock.

Mary said, "It was like a war zone." Coming in from the interstate, cars were mangled; it was horrible, like a bomb had been dropped.

I stopped at Waveland Avenue and Route 90, and it was all full of National Guard and relief tents. I asked myself, "Who are these strangers down here?"

Every time I came down I did shoulder and hand massages on site. People so enjoyed touch. In Baton Rouge I also did massages to heal my pain.

Then coming back I was dealing with bureaucracies, SBA, trailers, housing, guarantees of living expenses, etc. Things weren't going to happen unless everyone was on the same page, same day, every day. If not, nothing got done. What I did was pitch a tent in the back yard. I found a mechanical dummy and put FEMA MAN on it and drove around for weeks with it in the passenger seat. Everyone called me FEMA man.

I was in that tent for about 2 weeks. It was getting really cold in the 30's. When I got up it was dark, no lights, nothing to do. I would go to sleep at 6:00-7:00 p.m., get up at first light, get coffee drive down to convenience store or Brian, my neighbor, would make coffee or I made coffee. After the article came out in the Seacoast Echo (local newspaper), people wondered if I was freezing. I stayed with some friends for a while. Then I went to Gene Taylor's (state representative) office, the next day or two and they told me I had a trailer. On Thursday night someone offered a trailer with slide-outs. I wanted it to go to a family; it had more room. I took the Fema trailer.

I carry on what to do each day. Think about rebuilding, still waiting for the Insurance Company, FEMA, SBA to make a decision. So I'm really in limbo because I don' t know what the future has in store for me. Do I rebuild? I'm zoned commercial. I can't do that until they do the new flood map. They have the building at an elevation of 20 feet tall.

Mary: So many questions...it's such a mystery what to do.

Arman: I don't know the right answers about what to do, too many unanswered questions, finances, the coast, myself! I was thinking of offering the bank so much money and staying, or foreclose on me and you can have this dirt. I'm someone who will take care of this dirt. There is no one who will take care of this. Do I build the same thing or what?

I am more at ease and calm with people around me a more giving person, giving of my time to people in need. Life's not fair. Play the hand your dealt. I'm not out of the game. When I find myself out of the game, I'll find myself a dirt heap. I'm not ready yet or even close to that.

Mary: This is an interesting thing. Right before this happened we really felt we were in paradise. We had fixed the house up, we enjoyed it so much we fixed the apartment up and rented it to a wonderful mother and daughter. We built the garden shed and really felt we had it together.

Arman: Brian felt the same way. He had two houses and had everything done. He was helping us get our stuff together.

Mary: Before the storm as I was sweeping the porch. Arman asked, "Why are you sweeping the porch?" Because I felt so good, felt happy, and content. It was so enjoyable to take care of a new painted porch. Taking care of something. I'll never regret that moment, to feel that contentment, joy for something you built, put your time and energy into.

Arman: Twice since the storm people said they envy me. "You don't have anything to carry around with you, I envy you, my house is off its tracks, has mud and mold slime growing up the walls. You have nothing."

Mary: We are constantly having to let go of things, tools, videos, music. It is hard to stay in a place of trust, but it becomes possible as photos we had lost are returned from friends.

Arman: My needs and desires are more focused on the bigger picture.

Musings

"Your unhappiness ultimately arises not from the circumstances of your life, but from the conditioning of your mind."

--E. Tolle

There is a bigger picture than the devastation of Katrina, something beyond the feeble attempt of bureaucracy to solve problems. There is something so deep within our core that is screaming to come out. Pema Chödrön talks about it in her CD, *"Getting Unstuck."* She tells the story of an interview with the Dali Lama. The interviewer was a psychotherapist named Cutler who met with the Dali Lama over a period of years and together they wrote the book, *The Art of Happiness.*

> One day during a discussion on guilt and shame the interviewer asked the Dali Lama, "Do you have anything in your life that you feel bad about that you've done?" The Dali Lama says, "Many things. An elderly monk came to me and asked about doing these yogic practices which require a lot of physical exercise. Designed for 18 year olds. I advised him against it because I thought he was too old. He seemed to take that well and he left. Then I heard he committed suicide. He committed suicide because of his belief system. He thought if he committed suicide he'd get a younger body and then he could do the exercises." So the Dali Lama was left with regret, that he unintentionally had been responsible for this man's death, this man's suicide. The interviewer was stopped in his tracks and asked, how did you ever get rid of that feeling? The Dali Lama paused for quite a while and thought about that and then he said, "I didn't, It's still there. I just don't allow it to drag me down and pull me

back." We have this idea that you have it or get rid of it. That question came from that point of view. Chogyam Rimpoche use to talk about this "being able to hold the sorrow of the world in your heart, while never forgetting" what he called the great eastern sun, which is the big vision, the bigger perspective. The global perspective. The sense of unlimited time and space so some sense of being pierced to the heart by your own suffering and the sufferings of others and of your own regrets without it driving you down.

Then he said, "I realized by being dragged down by it or held back by it would be in no one's benefit, not mine or anybody else's. So I go forward and do the best I can." Which is pretty damn good (says Pema). I believe we could all feel that he is the great teacher. He is and communicates the way he does to unlimited audiences that have no background in the way he was trained, no Buddhism, right across the boards. You could see he has his own things. It's not like he is untouched, has no sadness, no regrets. He just doesn't turn it into what we call *guilt*.

This negative shame drags you down and makes you feel bad about yourself and basically you become very powerless to help yourself, or anyone else. It is unhelpful to stay in that. We are not trying to get rid of something; we are trying to stay and that pierces you to the heart, humbles you, awakens compassion, actually makes you more tender and more you.

Those of you that experienced great grief know that grief can reach a point where the grief is so strong you can walk around the world and look at people and there are no filters, just completely open, You've been so reduced by your grief that you have no more cocoon.

That is actually a very bitter sweet experience because the grief is there and doesn't feel good. But on the other hand it is opening you to your world and you feel a tremendous tenderness for everything.

--Pema Chödrön

"A Silent Killer"

A family of three stayed 12 hours on the roof of their home to be safe from the storm. A nine-year-old boy named Matthew, his mother Angie, and his grand mother Paula lived in Pass Christian, Mississippi. Katrina happened at the end of the month. People paid monthly were at the end of their pay period and were short on cash. This affected many people's ability to leave.

Angie: We stayed because of me. I was between pay days and had no more money. This house survived Camille and was made of concrete.

Paula: We should have gone to my sister's house.

Angie's story:

Before the storm, I asked a friend of mind who reads tarot cards in Biloxi, what she thought. She threw the cards down, and what she saw scared her so much that she didn't look at them for a while. Now she won't do readings over the phone. She said, "It is really going to be bad." I said, "You've been wrong before." She replied, "I'm not wrong this time...it scares me."

I had been lighting St. Michael's candles for six months. I always kept one lit; as soon as one burned out I'd light another one. I lit it the night before the storm and put holy water over the house, when I heard what she said about the cards.

I should have known when Mike R. left, I should have left. The house was built like a bomb shelter. The house was made of concrete and rebarb. In that house, if it was cold outside, it was cold inside; if it was hot outside, it was not hot inside. The houses that survived were concrete. I couldn't afford to leave; I didn't think it would be that bad. I couldn't see where 20 feet of water would go. My brother made a joke when he left for the storm. "You'll probably only have a foot of water in the house. I'm going to leave the homemade ladder for you." He was nervous.

Our belongings were close to the house, or in the house, but the house was under water; we had 30 feet.

Up to the time the storm hit, St. Michael's candle was lit. We (mom and I) were arguing because she blew out the candle. I said "you snuff it out." When the candle went out, the outside water was up to my knees. There was no water in the house yet. My friend who read the cards visualized us and saw us arguing when we got disconnected on the phone. She said we would survive it, it would be rough. She had a cop friend look for us afterwards.

We heard someone next door at my brother's house, looting on that street before the storm. I could hear them outside my window. Thank God they were there; we might have drowned in our sleep if they hadn't woken me up. They were two men, and I said they have to be looters. It might have been angels in disguise because I never went back to sleep; instead, I stayed awake. About 3:00 a.m. I put the TV on. It was raining outside. The power went out about 5:00 a.m. I knew the hurricane was here when the power went out. I was up, Mom and Matt were asleep, I got a bucket, climbed on it, and I looked out. I said, "Oh my God, water is everywhere, we are surrounded by water." I couldn't open the front door because of the pressure. The windows were the old roll-out style. I couldn't get out. The only way to get out was through the back door. While the baseboards blew from the inside of the house, Mom went in the bathroom and saw the sewage backing up and overflowing in the tub and toilet.

I said, "We have to get out right away." I had called my brother in Baton Rouge and told him water was coming in the house. He said "Take three suits of clothes, food and groceries in a bag." Matt put clothes in his book bag and put it on his back. I was going out to put bags higher up on the refrigerator outside. I knew the water was going to come in. I could see panic in Matt's face. I told him, "You stay here. I have to go out and put bags up high." When I opened the door, there was not much of a resistance. When I went back inside, I told Matt, "You have to get on top of the car with Mom." That was the plan.

The water went from my knees to my waist, up to the windows of the car in about 20 minutes. We are right behind Poctache Bayou and the gulf, and it was coming so fast you didn't have time to think. You never would have known the hurricane was coming because it sounded like rain, like a silent killer.

After I put Matt on the top of the car, I told Mom, "You and me have to go get the ladder. I climbed over the fence. The water was up to my waist and the bottom felt mucky slushy, like a bayou, and impurities came with it. Some people say hurricanes cleanse the water. I don't know. I lost my shoes climbing over the fence. The pressure of the water pulled the fence down. I told mother to pull the ladder. She never questioned me. She just did what I said. It just came to me what to do; it wasn't pre-planned.

Later when we were in Baton Rouge, LA we met a woman who was psychic and she said to Mom, "you left the house when you were meant to. She said St. Michael was with you." She told mom to get a statue of Michael. She was at Ryan's Steak house and she said we would see her again, but we didn't go back.

Matt was on the car, and we put the ladder along the house. It fit. Mike built it tall enough. I went back to get Matt, and the water was up to my waist rising quickly. I was scared Matt was going to drown. Mom had a purse with important papers, medication, and her cell phone in a zip lock bag. Matt told her to get organized the night before, and she put it in her purse. Mom was afraid to come up the ladder. She is scared of heights. I went back to get Matt, and he went up the ladder. I went up, and then Mom went up and didn't question anything because the water was rising very fast. When we reached the roof, I pulled the ladder up and laid it there with us. Matt had a Game Boy, games and clothes in his book bag. I had a purse, Mom had a purse, plus a black garbage bag she told me not to let go.

We started to see the refrigerator float down the street, so I knew our clothes and food were gone. Tornadoes started at 9:00 a.m., and I looked at my watch and timed the storm. It kept up till 9:00 p.m. It sounded like a train. I've been in hurricanes all my life, and I've never heard winds that fierce before. When I was putting Matt on the car, the water was coming into the house, and it was getting deep. The deep freezer was floating, and I had to push it out of the way. It was blocking the back door.

When we were on the roof, I was holding on to Matt, and he was holding on to me and my mom. We were all holding on to each other. There was this little metal pipe protruding out of the roof over the bathroom; we were holding on to it. I was holding on with one hand to that, Matt with two hands on me and Mom two hands on Matt. There was a time when we got lifted up off the roof. We just held on to each other. All around us we could hear the trees snapping, or uprooted always in an opposite direction from the house. We knew when the tornadoes were coming. I kept my back to the wind the entire time. I told Mom not to look, to keep her back to the wind. She looked and a piece of bark went in her eye. While we were on the house, it shifted three times, like it came off its foundation. I was very aware of everything, even the smallest details. I was never alert like that before. Mom was like a puppet. She didn't know what to do. Things just came to me. I just knew we had minutes to get out.

When we were on the roof and I had never seen so much water in all my life, we could see that both of the cars were under water. I was measuring the depth of the water by what I could see. I could hear electrical lines crackling. When we were on the roof, a tree kept slapping us on our backs as if it was telling us to move, as if it was saying "I'm coming down." But we didn't move; we stayed right there. The water washed the roots of the tree, and it came down. This big white oak tree fell on the house five feet from us. We heard the snap, crackle and pop. The tree took up the whole roof. That is when we found that the roof was safe. It was concrete about eight inches under the shingled roof. With a tree that size any other roof would have collapsed, and we would have fallen through. But it was concrete, so we were safe. I felt we were safe. I never stopped to think we were not going to survive. The card reader said we were in a bubble, protected the whole time.

The tree came down, and we stayed on the roof. I saw the water at the edge of the roof, and we had to go higher into the tree. We lost the back of the roof when the tree came down. I lost the ladder. Soon the back deck and garage collapsed.

When the tree fell the house never moved off its foundation again. The tree saved our lives. I told Mom we needed to go up the tree. The water climbed up to the edge of the roof. I never saw so much water. I'm looking at other houses, the whole time trying to measure the depth of the water. It was like a gigantic washing machine; there was no current. It would swell, just constantly coming up higher and higher.

The water started coming over the roof. There was a fork in the tree. I put Matt in the tree and held on to him for dear life. I told Matt to hug the tree. I told Mom to climb up the tree. She refused to. She said her hips were locking up. She waited until it came to her waist on the roof. She handed me the black garbage bag and said, "Don't let it go." Her purse is about 20 pounds now. I told her that if the water comes up, I can only save Matt because she can't swim. I told her to climb over and let her shoes go. That's how she got up the tree. We're all on the tree, Mom's further away. I dragged this big piece of deck that had been floating in the water to get higher in the tree. Matt started crying.

I told mom to go higher. She was crying, the water was over the entire neighborhood, and I could only see two roofs. We watched a boat float down the street and thought about jumping in it. I watched it capsized, so glad I didn't do it.

We're in the tree watching this big skid, the water was moving with three foot waves pushing the skid back and forth. The water was swelling, and the skid was being pushed toward my mom. I told Mom, "You have to go up higher to be safe." I'm watching her feet, and the water came all the way to the bottom of her feet but it didn't come any further this time. The wind pushed the water. Some say the wind came first. I have nightmares about the water every day.

When the water was starting to go back, we went from the tree to the roof, but we couldn't get off the roof. The ladder collapsed with the back porch. We were stuck there.

We were on the roof from 9:00 a.m. Monday till 10:00 or 11:00 a.m Tuesday morning. I got off at 9:00 a.m., but Matt and Mom did not want to come down.

The tree on the roof provided stability for the house by holding it down. It provided shelter for us. Matt and I slept in the tree where the tree forked off about four feet up. During the night the water took three hours to go down. As the water drained, wood landed on the roof, and I made a tree house for shelter. Hypothermia set in. I had a big piece of plywood that stayed up and put the sheet of wood over our heads. We stayed under it during the rain. Three 2 x 4 planks lay on the tree branch. Mom slept there. Matt slept under the tree limb. The big tree was a wind breaker. I slept in the hole.

I had made a quick patch on the roof with tar paper the week before because the landlord would not fix it. I ripped the tar paper off and put it over us for protection. It was a good thing we had the roof patch. We used some of the tar paper from the roof patch as a blanket from the rain.

We came down when the water went down. You feel like an ant. You realize how small you are. I saw a little squirrel about three feet from us as he hung onto the tree for survival. The tree was so huge all kinds of things stuck up there. While the water was up we saw houses float into the street. When the tree came down, my brother's house broke off its foundation and floated into the street.

The lady next door had plants on pieces of her deck. It was hanging over the edge of the house. I went over there to see if I could pull it onto the roof the next day. There were slats in the deck. I thought, if I could get this deck pulled over here, I could make a kind of ladder and we could get down.

During the night we saw helicopters flying over. When the water went down, helicopters were flying over the neighborhood. They did not help anyone. There is no way they couldn't have seen us, with Mom's underwear flying on the roof.

The most beautiful sight was daybreak. However, when we woke up, the sun was up and it looked like Vietnam.

Mom said she never slept that night. She literally spent the night on the tree limb.

The whole time it was freezing up there, and hypothermia was setting in. I couldn't stop shivering. Mom would say, "St Michael, St. Michael please give us a breath of hot air." Then I'd warm up. She did it all night, and it blew the carbon monoxide away from us. There were gas leaks all over, at least four I could see, bubbling as houses moved off their foundation.

Mom prayed. She got cramped up at one time, and I switched places with her in the tree. Matt was hungry; I told him when we got down, "you better not miss a meal."

We could see people looting; some had night vision goggles. The man who tried to help us said he lived next door, where my brother lived. He said that he would help us off the roof and take us to the police station. He told us to jump off the roof. He lied. During the night we heard gun shots from different areas after the water went down. I said, we need to get off the roof in the morning because there were gas leaks. It was a dangerous situation.

We dragged the deck over the roof, Mom and I. It was about 60-70 pounds, but it dropped to the ground. So now the only way to get down was to climb down the oak tree. So I climbed down. The whole time the storm was going on my mom said, "My son is going to have a nervous breakdown when he sees his house."

I picked up the deck and angled it toward the house while a Vietnamese man helped me get Matt down. The Vietnamese man grabbed Matt and eased him down. Matt was scared to death. He was afraid of heights, too. Mom and Matt wanted to stay up on the roof. Mom said, "They will come get us soon." They never came.

On the roof there was a time I was drinking water from the sky, and it was salty so I stopped and spit it out. I heard you could go crazy drinking salt water, plus it dehydrates you quickly.

So the Vietnamese man who helped Matt down, lived at the end of the street and asked me how his house survived. I told him I didn't think it was there.

This is how it looked as the water rose. The houses were there physically. As the water went down, there was just rubble, bricks, like pieces of a jigsaw puzzle, like a washing machine cycle. The water was making waves, like lava lamps. I never saw water like that. Swelling, moving huge four foot waves, then you'd see a hole where the water should be. Then it would move down differently. There is no way anyone could have survived swimming in that water. It was like the movie *The Perfect Storm*, very similar, though not as deep. Five to seven foot swells, then it looked like a hole in the water, like the water was empty, then it came up again.

I helped mom off the roof and we were standing in muck about two feet deep at least, and glass was everywhere. I took a peek in the house. I said to Mom "We have to walk." I found two shoes to wear that didn't match. We were climbing over toothpicks of lumber everywhere. I saw fish in the ditch off of Cedar Lane that were still alive and saw dead fish on the roof before we got down. We were so dirty. We started walking toward the tracks. We were depleted of fluids and weak. We got to Cedar Lane, close to the tracks, and there were thirteen feet of lumber on the railroad tracks and to the north. It was incredible. We saw another man. All he had of his home was a picture. We had walking sticks to help us along the way. We walked over the tracks. We were going to the police station. It wasn't there, and we couldn't get over the lumber. I said, "Let's go to the beach." It was safer. A helicopter followed us the entire way. I went for a bath on the beach. I saw the bottom of the water, it looked clear. I took my clothes off and bathed in the water. Matt took his shirt off, and I waved at the helicopter. My feet were much better. We started walking along highway 90 and saw other people. They had the same idea, to go south to the beach. I saw a guy on a three wheeler on the beach. He gave us water for Matt. The guy said, "I'll come back and take you to town," but the three wheeler was sinking so I said, "Don't bother."

There was only one house standing between Hancock Bank and Miramar, the nursing home. Along the way I found a bottle of water and drank it. God provides. I found a two liter Diet Coke still sealed and a bottle of raspberry water. Everything was provided for; it was incredible. We were so much luckier than others.

I felt like I was in complete control; the only other time I felt like that was when I had a near death experience during a car accident.

My brother thought we were dead for a week. He was very upset. My cousin, a fireman, checked the house and couldn't find us.

At St. Paul's, we thought we found a place to stay for the night, but they said no. Cindi, a Pass Christian police officer, took us to the Long Beach shelter at Quarles Elementary. We were there for two nights. I had acid burns on my legs, and I stepped on several nails. Mom stepped on glass. I couldn't walk. I needed medical attention and couldn't get it here on the coast. There were no doctors. Then my brother found us and took us back to Baton Rouge where he lives. We stayed for five weeks, but I will never depend on family again in a time of need. Mom called a friend from Diamondhead, and he took us to the Espy shelter, and then we got to tent city, the Village, in Pass Christian.

A part of me feels material things are not important. I feel fortunate we could just walk away. I felt a big letdown from my family. If they cared about us, they would have taken us into their homes, no options.

I felt as long as we stayed together, we would survive. I felt stronger that we stayed together.

I was in control the whole time. I just knew what to do. I can't explain it. I don't know. I know we were protected the whole time. Life is precious and too short.

I would never go through another hurricane again.

Paula's story:

I stayed because of my daughter. She said when the kids were little we always left. We didn't have the money and we didn't even comprehend the water was coming in the house.

I've lost a lot. I am 58 years old and there is no way I can replace what I lost. School pictures of my children and graduation pictures. I can't get them back. Pictures of my mom and dad. My mom is 94 years old. I lost my graduation ring. I saved my ex-husband's picture. It was a Polaroid and survived. The Blessed Mother and St. Anthony in the shoe box can't be found. I know now if I ever get myself together, I'll never go through another hurricane.

Angie is very quick to think. I was praying to St. Michael and it was so awesome. A puff of hot air would come through for about twenty minutes. And then Angie would say we need cold air too because of the gas leaks, so I would pray for cold air.

I really truly believe God was there with us and St. Michael. I could feel him there. I could feel his presence. If someone had not been there that water would have kept rising. When we got on the roof, death never entered our minds.

I really could not get up that tree. I am scared to death of heights. I'm not a tree climber. When I was seven years old I climbed a pear tree and couldn't get down. Someone had to get a ladder and get me down. My hip went out and it locks up. I had a charlie horse in the other leg. I couldn't believe this was happening during a hurricane.

I had storage in one bedroom. I had all my stuff in tubs and all the tops came off, and everything was thrown around like a tornado. There is mud and muck all over.

I feel like now when there is a storm, take pictures, important papers, memories, important things you can't replace. People put their lives in jeopardy to stay. God helped us for a reason, I don't know what it is. He had a plan for us. I don't know what it would be. I think he kept a lot of people. He has the power and can take you if he wants to.

When the storm passed and I was awake, they were asleep, I saw the stars and I blinked my eyes, I never was that close to the stars before.

Matt's story:

I never got to go out the door first. My mom got the ladder from next door, and she lost her shoes. I lost the big flash light and umbrella. We went on the roof with my heavy book bag, Gran's heavy purse and mom's light purse. I was scared to go up there.

Up the tree, I cried. We got on the roof and held on to the pipe. Once the water was coming up, when the tree fell down, the house shifted three times. I didn't feel it. I wasn't really paying attention. Gran kept looking back; I told her not to.

Paula: The next thing, down comes the tree and half of the roof fell off where the back porch was. It was like we were in a bubble all protected by St. Michael. Protected by the man upstairs.

Matt continues...When the tree fell, I went up and I was the first one, Gran was second and mama was last.

Mom got a deck so she could put it on the limb, so she could be on the branch and not fall off.

The temperature was cold. Everytime there was a breeze my leg hairs was sticking up.

I had pine bark and sap in my hair, and bugs and chiggers in my ears. Angie says, "He was literally sleeping under the limb of the tree."

Three hours later the water went down. When it got dark there were looters in the neighborhood. I kept trying to play the Game Boy, but it wouldn't come on.

People had shotguns. The helicopters would not pick you up and help you.

Next day the helicopters went by and did not help us. I made a joke about this, laughing.

Made my own bathroom. The next day finally my mother got a deck, Mom and Gran dropped it on the ground. They dropped it in front of the house.

My mom climbed off the tree and God knows what she's walking in. She got the deck and put it in front of the house, so we could get off. We walked to downtown Pass Christian, and I think I was day dreaming. I was a little delirious. I was walking faster than Gran and Mom.

We went to Hancock Bank, and we went to the shelter. I think I'm never going to do that again even if my mom stays.

Everybody should learn this lesson.

Matt's Picture

Musings

Quantum Physics and its study of subatomic particles shows us that at this very deep level the particles have no meaning in isolation and could be understood only through their relationships. According to Lynne McTaggart in *The Field*, what this seems to say is, "The world at its basic level exists as a complex web of interdependent relationships, forever indivisible".

We are all connected to each other, and have trouble existing without each other. We connect on a level that goes beyond culture, race, gender, ethnic background, geography, ancestry, astrological birth sign, etc. In fact, all of these determinations happen to separate us and that is passé. Only the actions and words and deeds that connect us will work in this 21st century. Take a look around and see for yourself. What works and what does not? Go inside and see what feels right to you. Begin living as if you believed this. How would you feel, think, act, speak? If you want some examples in action come and see for yourself the unconditionally loving relief workers who have come to the Mississippi Gulf Coast to unselfishly help their fellow human beings.

Some of the scientific community is finally coming around to the same beliefs that spiritual traditions and the healing arts have had for centuries: that we are all one. In my doctoral thesis, I suggest we are all specks of light, and together we make up one huge light body. And at the very core of our being we have "Love without fear."

Living		**F**alse
Our	Without	**E**xpectations
Very		**A**ppearing
Essence		**R**eal

Maybe in this new century we are waking up to the very essence of who we are and beginning to live that in our daily lives. Maybe it takes a tsunami or a hurricane to jar our memory.

"I Like Change"

Deborah Lee Emery moved to the Coast from Birmingham, Alabama in 1985 and bought her first investment property along with her home. She works in the English Department at Mississippi Gulf Coast Community College and lives in Biloxi, Mississippi. She went through the storm with her fiancé's son Kevin Abraham, 20 years old who videotaped an hour and forty-five minutes of the storm as it progressed from wind to flood to the destruction of her home. His footage with humorous commentary shows the water rising from the beach, up the street, into the yard, then into the house and finally up to the attic as the house collapses. It shows the porch on the house across the street coming off and that house floating and crashing back and forth into the house next to it. He had never been in a hurricane before. They had to climb to the attic as her house filled with water. The debris came inside with the rising water, the downstairs began to break apart and the attic studs they were sitting on gave way. Moving to the other part of the attic was only temporary. They finally jumped onto a section of a tongue-and-groove platform floating by (which she recognized as her kitchen ceiling) and thus escaped the collapsing house. Her cat that hunkered in the attic with them was left behind during the rush to escape and was thought to be dead. Fortunately, he was found eleven days later, although traumatized and dehydrated. Five months later he finally seemed normal.

I stayed because I had stayed for all the other hurricanes. My sister was calling me, crying, begging me to leave. I checked with the neighbors to see if they were staying. They said they were staying. I thought about leaving, but I detest waiting in traffic. I had animals. Up to the last minute my friend Betty Sue called to see if I would go with them. I had the TV on the whole time while I slept that night. I didn't have a clue it would be that powerful.

When the water was coming in I said, "Oh shit, more work." I didn't like our life; we had gotten way over our heads with labor. Even friends said we worked too much. Twenty years of labor, working for retirement, but losing our life enjoyment in the present. We had a duplex we redid ourselves, my house, a rental next door--a total of six rental properties we fixed up. We were way over our heads in work. Furthermore, our contractor ripped us off on our house, took our money and did a bad job. My fiancé Brian and I were trying to build old and new together and the project had at least three more years to complete, if we were lucky.

So, there was a sense of relief not to have to repair anything; it was gone. When I was on the roof, I said, "Good, no more projects for Brian and me!" The next thing I remember saying was I had too much shit anyway.

Then after the storm we were in survival mode. I reflected on my travels in Europe when I was young and living in near survival conditions. I also remember thinking about all the rubble and trash everywhere and how much stuff we Americans accumulate. I vowed to reduce my intake of "stuff."

In the aftermath, I neither cried nor mourned the loss. The influx of friends, family, and strangers coming with open hearts and full hands filled me with so much joy and gratitude that there was no room for grief about things. There was no way to feel sorry for yourself with such an outpouring of love that still continues to come. It is so wonderful. I never grieved about losing things. Observing my fiancé and others cry, I sometimes wondered at my lack of emotion over the whole thing and studied myself. I realized that for some time I mentally avoided picturing myself walking through the house the way it was. I didn't allow myself to go there. Maybe out of fear of depression. I just saw it as it was, destroyed, and then I came to grips with that. As time passes, something special will come to mind that is gone, and I feel sad that it is gone. Later, I felt sorrow over special items like the art work, much of which was very personal because it was produced by my sister, daughter, friends or myself. I wish I had these sentimental things like my collection of handmade jewelry. I'm sorry it is gone but other than that, I don't hold onto those thoughts. Trying to make the best out of what we have and be thankful, I think I will be okay. I'm an Aquarian; I like change. Otherwise, I am so busy with the "now" of insurance incompetence and FEMA and daily living there's no time for the past.

I think the value of friends and family have always been important to me, and the wonderful strangers that gave and gave with their hearts and they are still here. I reflect about how I have all these projects and don't have time to get away or help others, which makes me appreciate these people's giving of their time. I just see these people living their belief (Christians) and it makes me want to belong to a church.

With devastation comes uncommon events. I was fortunate enough to go to an Anthony Robbins' seminar in Palm Springs, California ($5,000 per person). Twenty-six Katrina victims from the Mississippi Gulf Coast and New Orleans were given an all-expense paid trip to Anthony Robbins' *Date With Destiny*. We attended from December 2 to 9th. It was 6 days of the most incredible life-changing seminar that I've ever attended. Everyone changed because of it.

We have lost 20 years of hard work and investment. It has been frustrating dealing with adjusters, FEMA, SBA, and the incompetency of each of these entities. Their errors constitute extra work, frustration and stress on our end and constant checking on the status of their work. I am tenacious so I get results. I wonder how the elderly and the less assertive people fare in all of this trouble. Everything is a waiting game. We are more than a little scared about the costs of rebuilding, but we feel sure we can weather this too.

Musings

The Guest House

by Rumi

This being human is a guest house.
Every morning a new arrival.

A joy, a depression, a meanness,
some momentary awareness comes
as an unexpected visitor.
Welcome and entertain them all!

Even if they're a crowd of sorrows,
who violently sweep your house
empty of its furniture,
still, treat each guest honorably.
He may be clearing you out
for some new delight.

The dark thought, the shame, the malice,
meet them at the door laughing,
and invite them in.

Be grateful for whoever comes,
because each has been sent
as a guide from beyond.

"Getting out of Dodge next time"

Cathy Brugger has been in Mississippi for 15 years. She came down with her mom and dad when they moved here. She and her husband John Volkman stayed at the Holiday Inn Express on Rt. 49 in Gulfport. John went in with the first responders.

I had to work at the Holiday Inn Express and we closed on Sunday night. I planned on staying at the hotel. I debated whether to stay with mom and dad, Diane and Tony Brugger, at Harbour Oaks Inn in Pass Christian as usual, but there were too many animals. I had two dogs and three cats, so we stayed at the hotel.

It seemed bad at the Hotel but we had no clue as to the strength. We got it as the water was just coming over Rt. 49 as the storm passed.

When I ran down the sidewalk to get the first-aid kit in case someone needed it, I stepped on glass. John ran back into the storm to the van to get surgical instruments out of Dr. Debora Zerr's car.

I ran to the lobby of the hotel. I had to go out around to the maintenance entrance. I know what tornadoes feel like from Tulsa, Broken Arrow, "tornado alley." I felt a tornado go over the hotel. We watched car windows popping left and right during the storm.

They took out a piece of glass half the size of a pinky nail embedded one-half inch into my foot. I still have problems today because of it. I am almost positive I have glass in my feet.

Since the storm, organization and routine are important for me. If I don't have it, I go nuts. I'm getting a little anal with it and driving John nuts too.

We watched a Burger King sign go by, saw traffic lights go. Almost got hit by the Burger King sign when standing by Dr. Zerr's doors. If I hadn't moved to the left it would have hit me in the head. Michael's bar sign went by.

We went in and out during the storm when winds were down. Tried to clear debris so it wouldn't cause any more damage. A cloth canopy broke windows in a truck because it was wet and kept smacking into it.

I remember we lost power at 5:30 a.m. and other people and my dad said something about it when I talked with him, so I think Mississippi Power turned it off.

That evening I rode with a friend to see what we could see. I couldn't get to the Pass. I felt I needed to get there and yet felt I didn't need to get there. That night I was put in charge of running the hotel.

On Tuesday morning, John, Dr. Zerr's husband, Bill and mom came in and told me about dad, how he died in the storm. I told mom it would be good to get to the property and get the dogs. Debris was piled 20 ft. high. I didn't know dad was covered with a sheet. I walked over the sheet a couple of times and finally picked it up and saw dad. I found Mattie and Truman (dogs) hiding under the roots of a tree. I used extension cords for leashes.

I found Scenic Drive cleared to walk and felt stupid. Got Truman and Mattie (dogs) and walked back to the car and went to the fire station and reported about our missing dog. I waited there and they called Rebecca Reispoli's radio. She was on her way to Biloxi with the dog. She brought him back to us. Harley didn't make it, figured he let go because he wanted to go with dad.

We stayed in the hotel for a week and it was like the Palace at Versailles. It stayed hot, nasty, and stinky. I had the door closed because of the animals (two dogs and three cats), and after the storm a fourth cat. There were three families.

We were cooking with two barbecue pits. The doctor made coffee in the fondu pot and we raided the hotel supplies.

I had booked out 50 rooms to Mississippi Power but only five got used. We had little groups who came in for disaster relief. Some locals needed a room and were there a week. I just gave her the room. Getting gas, getting money, getting cars fixed was difficult.

I got Mom to Mobile one week after the storm. We followed the next day. My aunt and sister gave us a duffle bag full of what we needed.

Then we drove to St. Louis. John came back to help with demort, funeral homes and morgues that pull bodies. He said in Hancock county alone the deaths were in the high 500's.

I've lost my dad and two dogs because of it and a lot of faith in any sort of system. It feels like we're on our own, only got my $2000 check from FEMA. They haven't called about a trailer and they denied rental assistance because they said I didn't ask for it. I had to appeal. I still haven't heard.

I learned I am getting out of Dodge next time. Do you think Zeta will come here? There is a tropical storm Zeta in the Atlantic right now. It's Winter!

Now I am trying slowly to pick up the pieces. John's got a great idea about a new business. He said he'd never leave Mississippi. I said I'd never move to California. San Diego looks wonderful right now.

"It Went from Bad to Unbelievable"

Kathy's mom and dad lived in Pass Christian and owned the 150 year old B&B The Harbour Oaks Inn. I spent many Mardi Gras parades and had several dinners there with Diane and Tony Brugger. During any storm they were always ready to feed and shelter the rescue workers, police, and fire fighters. Their hospitality is unmatched. I dearly miss Tony and his great sense of humor and loving way with animals. Diane ran the B&B like no other I have been to. She is a very gracious lady and was always trying to feed me. I miss her presence on the coast. The following are the words of Diane posted on a website about Katrina.

This will be brief, as every time I even start I have great difficulty getting past the second sentence. The night before the storm, we had the house clean, ready, and well supplied to take care of any evacuees the police might bring to us. Darlene, our housekeeper and I had been preparing food all day and throughout the night we were feeding the EMTs and police. As we were 33 feet above sea-level and Camille never made it into the house, we arrogantly believed we were safe. We took a brief nap at 3 a.m. Katrina had been taken down to a CAT 3. We were up at 5 a.m. and from 5:00-9:30 a.m. it went from bad to unbelievable. There were tornadoes and all of our plywood over the doors and windows were ripped off or blown out. We were in a 2nd floor bedroom, the one with the American Airlines bathroom.

At this point the surge came. We thought it already had come. The house started breaking up into four or five pieces. Both houses on either side were already gone. We were attempting to get to the billiard room to step out into the water when our apartment broke from the main house. We were in Tony's workroom at the top landing of the back stairs when the ceiling collapsed. Tony was caught in the corner and was taken down under the water. Tony's high craftsman tool chest fell on top of Mark, Darlene's husband and Tony's workbench and metal shelves fell on top and me and Harley. Darlene, how we'll never know, got the tool chest off of Mark and I was able to get out from under the work bench and shelves with Harley. I know Tony was already helping us. Ivan, Truman, and Mattie were already on top of the debris that Mark, Darlene, and I had just stepped out onto.

The debris eventually wedged into the three oak trees behind our apartment. I remember all of us "dancing" on the debris to keep from getting our feet wedged in it. It was here we lost Harley. Once in the tree, Darlene climbed up to the top, then Mark, then me. We intertwined fingers, toes, and anything into the vines to hold on. I was able to still "dance" on the top of the debris. We just had to be careful because the trees started to give away and the vines would loosen then tighten up again; afterwards, we saw a huge sink hole at the base of the tree we were in where the trees were about to fall. Those trees could have fallen so easily, but Tony was working hard, watching over us.

While in the trees I noticed spools of my thread wedged into the bark and thought about trying to extract them-I might need them later! By this time we were all in hypothermia. When the waters receded, it was so fastless then a half hour, I lost sight of the other 3 puppies. I thought I lost them. My stove was at the base of the tree. The bottom drawer was open with all the lids to my pans. Again, I thought, "Good, now I just need to find my pans!" Darlene and Mark, who suffered a 4 1/2 inch skull fracture when he was hit by a 4 x 4 -- I saw it happen, went to get help and I just hunkered down behind the stove to get warm and wrapped up in an old tablecloth hooked onto barbwire. Darlene and Mark came back with help and from that point on I was overwhelmed by the love, support, prayers, and blessings from those dearest to me to complete strangers. Ivan, Mattie, and Truman were found the next day and we are all together here in St Louis with my family. My daughter, Kathy and her husband John are also here with us and they are safe. And Tony is still with me, in spirit.

We are having a memorial service for Tony on October 15th at The Old Cathedral (in St. Louis, under the Arch) at 9:30 a.m. with a celebration of his life at my sister's home afterwards. The Old Cathedral is where Tony and I were married 37 years ago.

I don't know what I will be doing after everything is settled. I do know I want to visit each and every person who has been dear to both Tony and I. I promise to update the website as often as possible. Bless each and every one of you for your prayers and support. It's been an honor knowing you and to have you in our lives.

Musings

Long-standing traditions and grand old buildings leave imprints upon our psyche, and when they are gone we seem lost for awhile, searching for the familiar, the same old, same old. The memories are deep within and sometimes foreign to the conscious awakened state. Then something--a smell, a picture, a voice, a sound--will awaken the sleeping dragon and we are brought immediately to the familiar. A forgotten memory has been awakened. Sometimes we do not know why it is familiar, just that it feels that way. Other times we may wonder, "was it a past life or am I shifting dimensions?"

What will happen when the everyday things are completely gone and even the landscape doesn't resemble what we remember? I had an interesting experience just this past week. I went to visit a friend in Bay St. Louis; I had not yet seen too much of the destruction in that town or the remains of her home. I picked her up and we headed for the beach road. She kept pointing out what use to be in each location to help jar my memory and then I realized I hadn't even tuned into the landscape because it was so different from before. I could not get it. It was such a shift in consciousness. Nothing was familiar. How do I take this in? It took me several minutes to even comprehend what was happening. It was a shock that seemed to approach silently. I wonder how many times this happens in our life and we never become aware of the subtle shift and possible stress on our psyche.

Add to this the people, the animals, the trees, the shore birds all missing and I begin to understand what my friend up north said: the devastation is so great you can not take it all in. I couldn't recognize anything along that beach road. As far as I was concerned I was in a foreign land. I wonder how the tsunami people can get their mind around losing 140,000 people.

This wasn't the typical dissociation. I didn't go somewhere else; I was there, present and did not recognize anything. I get a sense of how mind control might work. I was told the other day that the lack of street signs here reminded a friend of mine of what the French Resistance did to the Germans during WWII. They not only removed signs to confuse the enemy they turned some around as in the sign pointing to Paris going in the wrong direction. Perhaps this confusion on the Coast is a form of strengthening our psyche. An example of this is having the flu that makes us so weak we have to go to bed and this bed rest then helps us get stronger and better. Can this confusion after the storm expand us to accept more things and not just the traditional old forms and be shaken to our core to add something new and different to same old, same old, and become stronger?

Squash plant growing out of the rubble

"Second Row Seating"

Gwendolyn Canon is a seventh generation Mississippian. She was born in Jackson and lived there 2 weeks. Her mom is Rosa Lee McCoy Canon and her dad, Jesse Cannon, commandeered to help rebuild the Coast after Camille. He was an engineer. Gwendolyn draws for ABC and teaches art at D'Iberville High School. She taught in the Delta before moving to Gulfport. Seven years ago she bought a home in the Pass on E. 2nd Street that friends of mine once owned.

We had the TV working. It was a small old model and it worked and kept a good picture the whole time. I was able to talk to mother. My electrician loaded my gun for me.

I left Sunday evening. I forgot to put water in the bathtub. I never forgot that before. Water, next to gasoline, was the most precious thing. I had a bicycle, aired both tires. I stayed and put all frozen food in the cleaned out refrigerator and left stuff here in my house. Had provisions. Had stuff in my car too. I had put some of the stuff in the car and packed up. All my stuff is okay. When I left my house I put my hand on my door and said, "I'm giving this house to God." I boarded and battened it down. No trees hit the house. The large tree out there-- I always say I don't want that tree to land on the house. The tree just fell down and bent in the opposite direction from the house. It's a miracle.

I stayed at 1402 E. 2nd. Street with Peggy Groves. It was such a loud storm. There was a certain smell with the water. It was horrible. It was in the high 90's and it stayed in the 90's. It was hot and no way to take a bath. Midday Sunday I got ready.

We would just hold our hands and just pray when we would hear the storm. We still have our cars: Kevin, Bill, Peggy, me and my son, and Robe Flory, who had been in Camille.

I wasn't scared during the storm. It was raining horizontal, everything was horizontal.

I had to crawl over trees to get out. Had to have big saws to cut the trees. That was the thing to do and what we needed to do. We ate well the first few days after the storm. We did all freezer food, had Filet Mignon. Then I had a generator.

After the water went down, people were just walking on E. 2nd. They were blown out of their houses. They were just walking to where they knew someone. Before we had water, before we had the National Guard, we had the news people.

Communication was so important. Couldn't call because cell phones wouldn't get out. At 10:00 p.m. that night after the storm I called Mother and she screamed and cried, "I thought you were gone." The news had us gone.

There is nothing that hasn't changed. The only thing that hasn't changed is the sky. The sky hasn't changed.

We all have a kindredness who rode out the storm. A lot of people are expressing the same things, for example, "Who needs a carpet any more?"

I can sit and cry, cry, cry. I had to take medicine to sleep and stop crying. I didn't sleep until recently.

Everybody's stuff was in the road. There were plastic bags wrapped around trees. I've never seen anything like this before. I've seen cars and wind and water before.

You couldn't go home if you have a house. For several weeks anyone who left for the storm could not get back into their Pass Christian homes. Got to stay if you have a house to take care of it. If you left the checkpoint the first couple of weeks you could not get back to your home.

Everything is different. They feed you free at the food tent in the Village. I've gained weight. I go there to see friends or meet people I didn't know. It is one focal meeting point.

We're going to make it, we know how to do that. I bought some pretty sheets to make it pretty where I am. Being together helps.

I stayed because they lowered the storm to a category 3. I taught for two years in the Delta. I started the Art Department at the Junior High in Clarksdale. I was doing both, here and in Clarksdale. It was the best of both worlds.

They said the hurricane was a category 3. It was a 10! The picture at St. Stanislaus looks like what I saw. Water was up to the porch. I stayed at Peggy and Bill Groves'. Bill and Peggy were staying; they had equipment to stay. There was a generator, a bigger house and it was brick. I don't have a generator, and I don't know how to do a generator or work a chain saw. So I was with friends who are like family.

We were busy getting things ready that morning, had TV on WLOX, and just listening and watching all day. Couldn't talk to anyone. Communication was gone. Could hear trees falling. They put cars under the front porch area, and you could get between them. Hurricanes have feeder bands and you can tell when they are coming. Every once in awhile we'd go out between the feeder bands. She hid her smoking. Peggy would go outside to smoke. We'd grab our hands and pray when it got bad. There wasn't any fear. I knew it was going to be okay. I had peace. I was totally at peace. I was actually enjoying it. Oh! No! Did that one get the house! Oh! That one went across the road! Oh! There goes Mr. Green! Get him in. He floated out his bedroom window on his mattress! He only had 6 inches in Camille, so of course he stayed and I could see out toward the beach from upstairs.

Before the storm I went to Bill and Peggy's. We ate okay because we grilled outside by the pool. Their house was big enough to have my own privacy. Watched news on TV, text messaged others, took pictures of the beach and harbor. I was totally calm and at peace, had no concern.

We woke up at 4:00 a.m. when Bill came downstairs and checked the generator. The wind started to blow, things moving around. They had plywood on all the downstairs windows and doors. We could see out of the top and in the back downstairs.

Water came in the window sills. It came in underneath closed windows. Kitchen wall was leaking and it was coming down windows so I was rolling towels and when I looked out I didn't know what I saw because it wasn't supposed to be there. I saw it but I didn't know I saw it until someone asked me if I saw the water. Then I knew I saw it. And I saw the roofs of houses, water up to the roof, things floating.

I was watching TV, calling on cellphone, rolling towels, I knew what was happening out there.

The storm was extremely loud. Could hear the trees snap. Same storm at 6:00 p.m. still going on but only about level 2. So we go out.

There weren't many people here. About five or six people were walking out of the storm. Paul Murrell from Spence wanted to go to the Stucco house on Shadow Lawn, so we started walking and I saw all the houses in the middle of the road and all kinds of people's stuff, walls of people's stuff, debris. I knew there were some bodies in there so I said, "I'm not going any further."

You saw material twisted, pictures, chairs, tool boxes, broken lumber, cloth, metal, plywood. Lots and lots of plywood. Teddy bears, toys, every once in a while see a plastic truck or slide. A grand piano upside down turned over upside down. Everything you could see was not okay, it was upside down or broken or part of something. It was messed up, not okay. That's when I went into shock. It is so surreal, it is still surreal. The trees are surreal. I hope they come back, they took such a beating.

First when I got terrorized, this is something I never dealt with. This is not supposed to happen. I played with tragedy, not dealt with it. The death of landscape, neighbors, birds.

The news people were here before the first responders or help.

The sound of the *quiet* is deafening because it was so loud. The quietness was worse then the storm, death defying quiet. No bugs, no birds, no wildlife, no crickets, no chirping. You'd hear helicopters, no police to come help. You'd hear dogs. Seven or eight years ago before I moved here I had a dream. I was looking out and saw water. There were four cyclones on the water and I would move west toward Pass Christian in the air like flying. When they came to the ground, they turned into four tractors with 18 row plows behind them going north and they plowed all the ground and houses up. It was tearing everything up. That is what water does, just like the plow. And I started repenting, asking God to forgive me for everything. It scared me. I called on God to have mercy. So I thought I'd be okay to come to Pass Christian. I took it as a sign that it was okay to come. Everybody who has come and helped me has been right there when I needed it.

How do you continue to live here when there could be another storm?

You'd listen and look for light and sound when the electricity was off to find out what was going to happen next. Everything was crazy after the storm, *hustle bustle*.

The last time I talked to Mother it was 10:00 a.m. After 10:00 p.m. I was able to talk to my mother and say I was okay. Then early in the morning 4:00 to 5:00 a.m. after the storm, you could talk. They went through the storm with us on the phone. They thought we were dead. TV had us dead.

I never heard Mother so relieved and everything okay in her heart. She prayed so hard.

One night I saw a light in the neighborhood and it was Ms. Dick. She said, "The Penthouse Apartments were on fire." They had trucks with buckets of water to put the fire out. It was sad. I watched them all night long. Tuesday night we had helicopters dumping buckets on it. The next day it rained buckets. Firemen worked Tuesday and Wednesday; they worked all day long.

We helped an elderly couple that first week. My son found someone in the rubble on Espy and he had died.

It's been horrific, surreal, dreamlike, still. As far as when we can be the same, there is no being the same here. It will never be the same.

I used to say, I would change every day and that would be the consistency of it. Who knows what I am? Every time I think I know about me and figure out who I am, I learn more about who I am.

I'm so much stronger. I could handle anything I'm supposed to do. I feel very confident. I know God is with me and I know there's power in what I say. If God is with me I can do all things. Through God I can do all things, through Christ that strengthens me. My biggest desire is to hear from the Lord. I need to be quiet and hear.

I've been horribly sad, I've never been so sad and upset. I've never had such streams of tears. The thing that is different, I cried and cried, I'm on medicine now so I don't cry.

The people who stayed are good people and those who weren't are now. I'm so grateful and thankful to have my house.

Dr. William (Doc) Canon was senator for 29 years. He resigned last year. He said if you help your neighbor you'll make it.

Love God with all your heart and love your neighbor as yourself. Have to love yourself first.

We were all falling around and tripping after the storm and more disoriented.

My dog stayed right by me and she would look up at the sky before she would go out.

We got the east side, not the eye.

My Uncle Billy said put a relief worker sign on your car and you could go anywhere.

My Uncle Billy in Columbus, during Rita, saw chairs flying around and he said watch the relief workers. If they leave, then you go.

I'm second row seating, being on 2nd Street, second road from the beach.

Musings

If we are curious and keep expanding, our experiences of change could be easier perhaps. When awareness is increased, possibly our shock factor is decreased. This is a possible scenario for tragedy. When the bigger picture is seen, the small details have less meaning. I had a recent example of this when I was accused by a friend of intentionally hurting her. This really bothered me; it triggered all kinds of feelings. Then when the friend said that she could no longer trust me because I intentionally hurt her, I felt a deeper pain from this situation. Each time it was mentioned or I even thought about it, I would go into this immediate reaction of being wronged or hurt or a victim of a false accusation. There was such a strong emotional charge connected to this. Then this past summer, August 27 to 30th, during Katrina, I was attending a seminar and retreat called *No Time To Lose*, by Pema Chödrön in the mountains of Colorado. Jessie, her assistant, taught us meditation practices before Pema's talks. We were shown how to use a direct experience as an object of meditation and this day we were to make the object of meditation something that *irritates* us.

> I chose what came right up in my mind which was this accusation of hurting my friend intentionally. I sat and nothing came. I labeled my thoughts thinking, thinking and my mind became clearer. I dropped into a calmer state and just allowed my inner knowing to let me find the answer to these strong reactions. I dropped below the storyline to find the deeper meaning. As I sat on my cushion and let go of any expectation, it all of a sudden came to me. The difficulty was me. I wanted to be *right* in this situation and the more I fought that battle the more I would be triggered and upset. Then an immediate calm came over me when I saw my part in this drama and the charge was no longer there. It was so simple to take ownership of the problem. What a relief I found. I thought of the situation again during the

workshop and the charge was gone. Well, six months later when I saw my friend, she brought up the situation. I found myself reacting with less of an emotional charge than before. The healing and letting go helped disperse most of the energy. I now have a practice I can use to help resolve this and other issues. The most important lesson is to own up to the part I am playing in a situation. The other piece is to have compassion for myself in the taming process.

The Blessings of the Fleet, Pass Christian, May 2005

"It's Like an Opposite Life"

Tu Phan is 16 years old and has lived the past 7 years in St. Martin, Mississippi. Before that he lived in Biloxi. He has lived all his life on the Coast. He is now working at the Blue Bell ice cream stand in Edgewater mall in the evenings.

My mom came over from Vietnam when she was fifteen and my dad was twenty when they met in California. I stayed during the storm with my mom, my older brother and sister and my younger brother and sister and my cousin. We wanted to evacuate but my mom waited for my dad to come in. He is a shrimper. He never came in, so after the storm we went to my cousin's house.

It was 3:00 in the morning and I pulled the blanket over me and my brother and it was wet. Water was ankle deep in the house. My older brother was still awake so he woke us all up. You thought you could get in a car, but we opened the door and the car was floating. We live by the Back Bay and it could have been worse but we had sandbags around the door and it helped a little.

We stayed there to 6:00 a.m. and we thought it wouldn't get any deeper; then it was waist deep. I have been through many storms. We just stayed there. When it got waist deep in the house we looked out and it was one foot over the window ledge and we live on a hill so it was a lot higher outside.

My brother and cousin went out the window to get help. It took them a really long time. I looked out the window and the water was two feet above the ledge. We got scared, so we decided to go where there was less water. We gathered everything we could. I was just in a tee shirt and shorts, and we had four dogs and five puppies. We took the puppies. My mom and everybody got into the room and everybody panicked and we were going to go back to the living room and get everything we could. The freezer fell over the door and we couldn't get out. It was full of water and heavy.

So we had to go out the window. In front of the house was a van and four cars. The van was right in front of the window. We were to climb out, and everyone got on top of the van and my brother and cousin were still gone. We stayed there five minutes and we were panicking because we couldn't find my brother and cousin.

My family was on the van. I was on my cousin's car parked behind the van. The wind was really bad. Pine needles were stabbing us.

I couldn't believed we stayed. I told my mom to leave but she was afraid my dad would come home and find no one there. We had a cell phone but it cut off. When it worked we called my sister's friend but they couldn't come because the water was too deep. Later on, he found the back way to come and get us. On Lemoyne, it was knee-deep.

We had bushes in the front yard. I swam around the bushes. Water was over my head. It was the deepest part because we are by the Back Bay. It is behind our house.

I saw my brother and cousin carrying a kiddy pool which floated by them. It was a miracle that they found the pool because my mom and sister couldn't swim. I helped them carry it to mom and my sister and brother on the van. We helped mom and my sister and the five puppies. The puppies were in a laundry basket with a trash bag so they wouldn't get wet. They were real small.

Then me and my older sister, younger and older brother and my cousin helped them pull the pool down the street swimming and pulling them.

There were fire ants in the water, lots of them. They were biting us. We had boxers and muscle shirts on. By the time we got halfway down the street I could tiptoe. Then we walked a little more and my neighbors were swimming out of their house and then we walked more and saw a family friend who parked on the street with water up half of the tires. He drove over the wire and branches. He was swerving and driving and the wind was pushing it. We got everyone and the puppies in the car. It was a two door Accord. We drove to my cousin's house who was with us that night.

My cousin and older brother were going to go partying around 10:00 p.m., but luckily they didn't. We went to my cousin's house in Ocean Springs and it didn't flood over there at all. We showered and stayed at his house. The electricity was off; we had candles. We got dressed and everything. We were really cold with wind and water. When we got in the car we were picking fire ants off us. We didn't care about the ants. We just wanted to get out of the storm.

We stayed there and talked about the storm to cousins and stuff for two to three days. We came back to the house to see if we could salvage anything. All the houses were down like tornadoes hit them. Everything was leveled, everything was to the ground. We never found our four dogs. We saw a coffin in front of a house in the middle of the street where a lady had died. We came back and got clothes out of the house. We were muddy and dirty so we wanted them.

We saw people that it only flooded a little bit and they were crying and sad and we lost our whole house and we didn't cry. We felt sad. Mom said, "Look at it that we'll start all over again. Look at it in a good way instead of bad way." We haven't heard from my dad yet. My mom was optimistic about it. We would be pessimistic and mom would say, "Move on."

One to two weeks after the hurricane, we had no electricity. We went around. My neighbor gave us water. The Red Cross gave us water. The electricity was still off and we got water from FEMA and the Red

Cross. We needed electricity and my Uncle owned a boat. It was okay during the storm so he went to his boat and got a generator. We carried it home. It only had a little gas in it, it only worked a little bit. So we had to get more gas. By this time we had clean clothes, we went back and forth to our house at least twenty times. We went to the house to get gas from the cars for the generator.

Then we got electricity from the generator and we were living okay. It was hot in the house. We were burning oil lamps before we got electricity. Our grandma was okay. She came over, talked to us and told us about her neighbor. She had stayed in the Buddhist Temple with her kids and other people and the water came up and they were swimming and it got up to the roof. They had about one foot of air and people couldn't swim. Some people died and were floating around them that they knew. I couldn't imagine seeing people I knew from church floating around me dead. We still hadn't heard from my dad at this point.

Our First Vietnamese Baptist Church over the tracks was brick. It was destroyed. It wasn't a big church but cozy. There were projects behind the church and trailers that flew into the church.

My grandmother's neighbor said to go up north, evacuate wherever there is electricity. My Uncle agreed with that. They all lived in the same neighborhood. My Grandmother and Uncle went to Chicago, but my cousins stayed and we stayed. My mom wanted to leave, but she hadn't heard from my dad so she stayed.

Everybody in the house stayed because we stayed; the other house left. We didn't have water or electricity and it was really hot. The day after the storm we slept outside and it was cool and breezy. You could see the stars. I've never seen that many stars in my life. It was really breezy, it was good. We were laying on top of the car and everything.

A few days or week or two my dad came back. He was really happy to see us. He came back to the house and saw it and was depressed, thought we were under the cars or debris. Then he drove to our cousin's house in Ocean Springs. He went to Texas to sell his shrimp because the storm was so bad. It just got too late.

A few days after we all went to stay with my Uncle 30 miles from Laurel, seven of us: me, mother, dad, older brother and sister and younger brother and sister and friend who came to get us and doggies. My cousin went to Jackson, gave one dog to a lady mom worked with, and one went to a cousin I lived with. So we had two puppies. We stayed outside of Laurel, Bay Springs for a while. My younger sister went to school there. I and my younger brother went to school in Jackson at Murray High School.

After that, it didn't work out because we didn't like living with others. Then we went back and forth to Bay Springs and Biloxi. Went to Ocean Springs Thrift Store. Next to it was FEMA and we applied to live on the cruise ship in Mobile and got accepted. It was nice and fun at first, only a few people, arcade, food was free. You could stay out as long as you wanted. In about a week or two more people came. Everything was restricted, 11:00 p.m. curfew. People were throwing ice cream at people who worked there. There were little kids who were loud and running up and down the hallways.

After the cruise ship we went to FEMA for housing assistance so we got off the cruise ship and rented half a house from a cousin with four bedrooms. Stayed two to three weeks then moved to Gulfport where we are now.

I've been through three new schools since the storm. It's terribly hard.

Before the storm I could wake up at 3:00 a.m. go to Walmart, 11:00 p.m. go to Taco Bell, took all things for granted. All friends, most of them are gone, some are still here.

Before I didn't think about problems. Now it's the past that's not that far behind, that's constantly present. The hurricane felt like a year.

Every once in awhile I think about all the fun in our house, a party every weekend. Now no party, no nothing, just sitting around. Hard to move into the new house. We had to buy new stuff. Started working one and a half weeks before Christmas because I wanted to.

Some things are different. My friends are the same. Objects, cars, TV, computer, and games are all gone. I miss my friends, this you can't get back. They are all over the states. I phone them sometimes but the time zones are different. When I'm going to bed they are awake, California, Oregon, Texas, Massachusetts, Tennessee, Florida, just everywhere! They all lived in Biloxi with me and now they are gone. We went everywhere together, some I didn't hang out with but they are friends. My friends in Biloxi are in houses that are messed up and some in trailers.

It's like an opposite life, to what it was to us. Things I had are gone. Things I experience now I never thought I could experience before.

I would evacuate for sure. But if my mom stayed or some of my family members stay I have to stay, I can't just leave them.

Musings

Because of Katrina many people are now scattered all over the USA. Ethnicity may become less important. We now have a greater diversity in more states then we had before. We now have the chance to expand our awareness of "other" as part of us. This can only change us for the good, if we begin to accept the idea of connectedness instead of separation. If we can see, feel, and know that deep inside we are all one, all a part of the God force, connected, with the same feelings, yearnings, how much better our country, our world would be. The outside container we choose to live in is only an illusion of separation. Our behaviors may be different and yet they are all changeable. Our spirit inside is the same and perfect without flaws. This is what we connect to when we dive deep into our souls. Going beyond the outside physical expression, language, clothes, customs, beliefs, etc. helps to expand our consciousness into accepting more and more of our oneness.

Pema Chödrön in *Getting Unstuck* suggests "opening to an unknown future as thrilling instead of as a threat." Just as Tu Plan's mom suggests to look on the positive side.

In *Start Where You Are*, Pema Chödrön talks about the following story:

> There was a Native American man called Ishi, which in his language meant "person" or "human being." He was a good example of what it means to be a child of illusion. Ishi lived in northern California at the beginning of the century. Everyone in his whole tribe had been methodically killed, hunted down like coyotes and wolves. Ishi was the only one left. He had lived alone for a long time. No one knew exactly why, but one day he just appeared in Oroville, California, at dawn. There stood this naked man. They quickly put some clothes on him and put him in jail, until the Bureau of Indian Affairs told them what to do with him.

It was front page news in the San Francisco newspapers, where an anthropologist named Alfred Kroeber read the story.

Here was an anthropologist's dream come true. This native person had been living in the wilds all his life and could reveal his tribe's way of life. Ishi was brought on the train down to San Francisco into a totally unknown world, where he lived--pretty happily, it appears--for the rest of his life. Ishi seemed to be fully awake. He was completely at home with himself and the world, even when it changed so dramatically almost overnight.

For instance, when they took him to San Francisco, he happily wore the suit and tie they gave him, but he carried the shoes in his hand, because he still wanted to feel the earth with his feet. He had been living as a caveman might, always having to remain hidden for fear of being killed. But very soon after he arrived in the city they took him to a formal dinner party. He sat there unperturbed by this unfamiliar ritual, just observing, and then ate the way everybody else did. He was full of wonder, completely curious about everything, and seemingly not afraid or resentful, just totally open.

When Ishi was first taken to San Francisco, he went to the Oroville train station and stood on the platform. When the train came in, without anyone really noticing he simply walked away very quietly and stood behind a pillar. Then the others noticed and beckoned to him, and they all got on the train to San Francisco. Later, Ishi told Kroeber that for his whole life when he and the other members of his tribe had seen that train, they had thought it was a demon that ate people because of how it snaked along and bellowed smoke and fire. When Kroeber heard that, he was awestruck. He asked, "How did you have the courage to just get on the train if you thought it was a demon?" Then Ishi said, quite simply, "Well, my life has taught me to be more curious than afraid." His life had taught him what it meant to be a child of illusion.

Let us become children of illusion and be more curious than afraid. Are the Mormons in Utah becoming children of illusion now that they are having native New Orleans residents doing Mardi Gras parades and second lining through their streets? Let us see the future as thrilling instead of a threat.

The colonel is wearing his bucket

Image is copyright of The Kentucky Fried Chicken Corporation.

"The Howling and Roar of the Wind"

Marianne Burkholder came to the Mississippi Gulf Coast in 1994 from Astoria, Oregon. She lives in Biloxi on Mauvilla Cove. She leaves for Alaska at the middle of May to salmon fish and she returns in the middle of August. Regina stayed with Marianne during the storm.

Regina Catalano came to the United States from Bolivia as a little girl. She lives in Biloxi, Mississippi and is a massage therapist as well as a translator for Spanish.

Marianne's story:

I had been through only one hurricane and I evacuated for it. That was Ivan. Since I am in Alaska every summer, I miss most of the hurricane season. My friend Emma Jane is who I usually evacuate with and I was going to go with her because she did not want to stay alone in her house. Then Regina called and said she wanted to go wherever I went instead of with her ex-husband. When Emma Jane's friend's home was too full I asked Regina to stay with me at Mauvilla Cove.

Saturday, one of the first things I did was go in the backyard and take all the pears off the tree and trim the branches. Then I boarded up some of the windows.

Regina called at 3:00 p.m. on Sunday when the wind began to blow and said she was coming over. She said, "Maybe I'll come now because it is getting blustery. " We both peeled and cut pears and cut them up for a long time.

Monday, looking out the back window the wind was swirling in all directions so you couldn't see. There was a constant humming and howling like a train in the distance. When big gusts came there was a huge difference. You could feel the wind build momentum. It felt like something was going to give like the roof and chimney. Something did hit the chimney.

When the gusts came it shook the house, climaxing with a roar. In pitch they were fairly regular. It was so noisy. The trees were going down all over, but all we could hear was the constant roar of the wind. In Alaska, the gusts from the gales were farther apart.

The first part of the storm was coming on shore and it came from the south in front of the house. The second half came from the Back Bay and hit the back of the house. That seemed stronger than the front maybe because we were here in the back of the house near the windows.

The hurricane force wind woke me up at 5:30 a.m., Monday morning, and I went into my healing room, where there were no trees nearby. Regina was already sleeping in there.

At 8:30 a.m. it was really blowing more and I thought it was the worst of it. I called mom at 8:30 a.m. telling her I was fine and thinking it was at its peak. But it kept up and got even worse after 8:30 a.m. The worst section was about a three hour period. It went on and on and on and you heard a constant roar. I was glad I was home because I got to see how the wind hit the house so I can prepare for the next time. By knowing the direction of the wind, I can prepare the house better. I lost three big trees to the hurricane.

I could hear water starting to drip in the living room so I moved all the furniture to the kitchen, got buckets, then heard it in other places--the den, bedroom, then leaking around the lights. In the living room you could see it soaking the sheet rock and the sheet rock finally gave way in sections until I was left with a 14' long hole in the ceiling. Our roofs would have made it if the storm hadn't been so large and taken around eight hours to pass over us.

In Alaska we have gale forces but the gusts let down; Katrina didn't let down. It had 120 mph winds. It was an exceptionally long time for that force of wind and gusts to last. It felt like the roof could blow off. I heard rattling around the chimney and didn't know what was going on around there. The ridge cap blew off. I could see light peeking through. It was weird at night to look up into the attic.

Electricity went off at 3:30 a.m. Monday. We turned on the battery operated TV at 5:30 a.m. I saw a light. Regina came to the bedroom. It was blowing hard. It was already at Point Cadet and Bay St. Louis people were asking for help because they had water in their houses. So this told me that it was really bad and it wasn't high tide yet. People were already on their roofs and were calling for help. But the rescue workers couldn't go out at that point because of the wind.

Regina went home on Tuesday. Wires were down and trees and electricity was off.

I didn't go anywhere till Saturday. I found clothes to take to others. They asked us to stay off the roads. They were moving people on Irish Hill Road at Michelle School and they said they weren't ready for clothes so I went to a distribution center on Highway 49.

Going to church was wonderful. One of the first things Jane said was, "The last three weeks I was preaching about getting rid of stuff and sure didn't mean this." So Tuesday morning we went to Regina's and found her house was fine, so she stayed there.

I had propane for barbecue and used a propane burner to make coffee. Went out on Thursday to go for ice. I cleaned out the fridge on Wednesday.

My neighbor had a generator for their dogs, which kept the motor home cool. I got my salmon in the propane fridge on Tuesday night while it was still frozen.

When the gusts came I'd visualize sitting on the floor in the healing room expanding my field and bring it up and out saying, God Bless Us, God Bless Us, God Bless Us. I wasn't afraid for my life. I heard the wind so strong. I didn't know what would give.

Sunday night we made pear sauce. I never ran out of food. I was content to stay home for a few days and I didn't need ice. I ate up hamburger and tacos, had lots of apples and almond butter and pear sauce and all the stuff in the freezer. I toasted millet bread on the BBQ with pear sauce. The weather was really hot but I was so content. I chatted with neighbors in their AC trailer to get cool.

Our home phone didn't work for a long time. Bernie, my ex-husband came by and said he got through to Blake, our son, at U of Colorado on Tuesday night and said that I was okay. He, Blake, called his grandma all day and talked for two hours on Tuesday while he waited for word from us.

It was weird to be so cushioned in here and see disaster on TV and what was right out the front door.

Regina and I walked down the street at 6:00 p.m. Monday night and walked halfway around the subdivision. We saw a neighbor who was only here one year, outside of his home by the water. I could just hold my hand on my heart and kept repeating, Oh, My God, Oh My God. He said he was staying on the second floor and it came up seven feet in his house, the tidal surge from the Back Bay.

He told the story that he wanted to get some water out of the cooler. So he had to go under the water at the door frame and his big dog followed paddling behind him. He saw his freezer floating on top of his car so he got it off. You could see he was in shock.

I asked my neighbor, who was putting a tarp on his roof if he could get my "shower curtains" over the ridge cap on my roof since I didn't have any tarps and no stores were open! The neighbors were great.

I guess I was never worried about anything; I felt you had to go through this to get to the next step of something. I already felt I enjoyed my days and valued them. I did feel all the pain and all the anguish going on. I did more praying to bring balance and calmness to the area. I asked guidance to bring someone into my life and home. I didn't expect what happened. The intention I was setting was to bring a partner in my life to share my home with me and it ended up different, with my ex and a friend staying with me. And it was fine because it was right after Blake left for college.

This brought it home again even deeper to do the work to stay balanced and centered. So as things go on around me, I stay grounded. It brought to mind the reading about walking the path with stuff and chaos going on all around and not being affected by it.

The other piece of that energy is that it's a weird feeling. An energy of anxiety and joyfulness mixed together. You don't know what's going on so you don't know what the anxiety and joyful feelings are about and you don't know what the future will bring so there are mixed feelings. Yet there is a bigger picture.

Regina's story:

The reason I stayed is I knew I needed to stay this time. I ran away twice and I knew I needed to stay. I knew it was going to be different than the two other hurricanes; inside I knew. The first two I was afraid of what I would find when I came back. Every time I left there was a sadness.

I had dreams before the storm about being in water with electrical lines around me and I didn't know what it meant. Basically I didn't want to go away with my ex-husband again and not be able to come back when I wanted to.

I didn't watch TV. I didn't know what was happening because I was getting the house prepared.

Marianne was not planning to stay. When she called back and said she would stay if I stayed, I finished preparing my house.

I've been in hurricanes before and some have been bad. There is a fear in the back of your mind, you might lose a roof, etc. I always feel a big sadness when I leave my house.

So I told Marianne I was going to be at her house 4:00 or 5:00 p.m. Sunday afternoon. I felt the feeder bands coming and the rain began coming. Feeder bands aren't constant, so it rains and stops and rains and stops. We got big drops. I knew it was going to rain more so I was getting nervous if it rained more I wouldn't reach Marianne's house comfortably. So I went to Marianne's and the worst part, I think, is to wait, watch TV, and watch it make landfall.

During the storm I wasn't nervous or scared. I had been through them before. I knew Elizabeth my daughter was safe with her dad and Gina, my other daughter, was safe in Memphis. It didn't occur to me that they would be worried about me. I knew I was safe. I knew in my head I'd be safe.

When it started, some of the worst part was the roar of the wind. The sound was different from the others I have been through. Most of the time when I meditated or prayed, I envisioned my protectors in the vortex around my house. Then I felt selfish and asked them to protect the whole neighborhood. I envisioned them as big blue beings with robes, arms and wings in a circle protecting us.

I don't think I was aware of the danger I was in. I think we both were very calm; we both kept ourselves centered. I think we handled everything as it happened. When the roof leaked we put out buckets. Put plastic down over the floor and took care of everything as it happened.

All the other hurricanes I ran away from talked about keeping water and ice, but it never had been as necessary to keep it as long as it was this time.

The learning for me was that if I had run away from it and had come back in two weeks, it would have been running away from something I couldn't face. Coming back to the neighborhood was like coming to a ghost town, no water or ice. You got close to neighbors that you haven't seen before in your life.

I felt I needed to experience it and opened all the windows. There was not one breeze. I said, "I can't stand this." Then I said, "I can." So I breathed and then I could stand it.

You also do appreciate nature. It was so silent and dark. I could see the stars. I could hear nature. To see nature and appreciating the sky and at the same time it was scary because of the darkness and total silence.

I kept thinking it was like the Planet of the Apes when I walked around and saw so much destruction and devastation. Or it was like a Sci-Fi movie where it is the end of the world and no one is left but you. Like the Body Snatchers, it was a horrible feeling. No one was in my neighborhood. No cars, no people and no stores open.

Then you began to see men in camouflage with guns, all emergency vehicles and Red Cross.

When I saw East Biloxi I thought I was in a war zone with the food distribution centers, Tetanus shots in tents, etc.

It's a mixed feeling to come to your house and neighborhood and find it almost normal and in East Biloxi it's a war zone. It is almost normal, but it will never be the same as it was, and we will never be the same. When they talked about the Earth Changes I didn't think it would come here first.

I think we will reconstruct and be better then we were before. Hopefully we have grown spiritually.

Musings

"What if, for the space of a year, we no longer waited for the seasons, what if we embarked on the most fabulous of journeys, what if, abandoning our towns and our countryside, we went on a tour of the planet?"

What if we understood that our borders did not exist, that the earth is a one and only space and what if we learned to be free as birds."

--Jacques Perrin, producer of Winged Migration

Nature stands before us in its magnificence and we are sometimes oblivious to it until it is gone. We have incredibly large, very large Live Oak trees on the Coast. Some are 500 plus years old. If they could talk, what stories they could tell. When I first moved down here, I couldn't believe how their branches just went on and on as if they were performing a graceful dance, touching the ground and then coming up again. I fell in love with them. Some of the old ones, if their branches were left untouched, provided wonderful seats for thinking or contemplating or just enjoying the view. I remember when Fridays put its restaurant on the beach and cut the branches of the oaks to make room in the parking lot. As I drove by I could feel the pain of the trees. I wondered what it felt like to have your arms cut off. They continued to stand stately in spite of our ignorance. And now many of those wondrous beings are gone and thankfully many are still standing. One day after they had opened the beach road to traffic, Route 90, I was cruising down the Coast and saw the trees. Now it looked like there were more trees than I had ever seen on Route 90. Then I realized my mistake. Even though we lost so many trees, they were more visible than before because most of the houses were gone on the beach road. All you could see was groves of beautiful oaks who had weathered this storm and many storms, standing together filling the landscape with nature's garden. I so enjoy the sight and am very grateful for their presence and beauty.

"Little Things Were a Big Triumph"

John McManus came to the Coast in 2001 from Philadelphia right after 9/11. His mother and sister live on the Coast. Bob Hammons, who is living with John, has been on the Coast for 56 years. They both were living in east Biloxi at Pearl and Kuhn in Point Cadet with four dogs during the storm.

I stayed because I'm hard headed. I survived other storms. I survived Camille and this wasn't supposed to be worse. *Oops, oops* is a good word.

Bob: It almost got us killed. We waited too long.

John: There is difficulty evacuating with animals. They don't want them when you check into a motel. I wasn't afraid of the storm. I didn't feel a sense of urgency until it was too late. I didn't have a sense of fear. The first thing I felt was how dare this nasty thing come into my house and destroy my things. Then I was afraid for the animals. The water came in fairly quickly. There was a pull to it, a current.

I guess the next thing I felt was a sense of frustration, not being able to get to anyone to help them. I heard people calling out and there was nothing I could do. It was either me or them because if I tried to get to them, I wouldn't make it. Thanks to Bob, keeping a cool head and getting the back door unlocked, we got to safety.

Bob: I went through the back window and got a couple of the dogs upstairs to the addition they were building on the house. It was an incomplete addition with only the frame. We stayed about two to three hours up there. We saw a house floating by and coming apart. We went into the attic of the house proper and rode it out there. We could see water in the house--it was about four inches from us. It was close, we could see it. It wasn't fun. I just want to forget it. Everything I used to remember is gone on the beach. Long Beach was my stomping grounds when I was a child.

The more I don't think about it, the more I can forget it. That's just the way I am. I wanted John to get out and he wouldn't and that's where I messed up. I wanted to leave the night before. We pulled the cars around in front of the house and I went in and told John I was leaving and the water came in behind him and we couldn't leave. It came in too fast for us to get out. About 9:00-9:30 a.m. I got hit by the car door; it blew and hit me in the face. But it was too late then. Winds were blowing since 2:00 a.m. or earlier.

John: I was on the porch for Ivan. The wind didn't strike me that it was out of the ordinary. But when the water came in my house it freaked me out. It was Bob's cool head that got us out. He went out the window and I had to go under water to get out. We were fine in the addition until it came loose and started to collapse. I went across the roof and tried to get the dogs into the attic from the outside. I became very acrobatic for a moment and got into the attic. It wasn't pretty.

Then Bob got into the attic and about two seconds later the addition collapsed. There was definitely some intervention that kept us safe.

Bob: There was a man up there protecting us.

John: I never felt I was going to die. Don't get me wrong--I was mortally afraid. I was more afraid for the dogs and Bob than for myself. Once we got to the attic I knew we'd be okay. There wasn't any concrete reason to feel that way; I just had a sense we were going to make it. I was pretty dubious when we were out on the roof and I wasn't in mortal fear.

After that I had Baby (dog) in the attic with me and I could see and hear Pudge and Ted and Bow (the other dogs). They were on the roof.

Teddy and Pudge wouldn't come in the attic and Bow was too far away to grab. Baby curled up with me in the attic.

The whole time the water was rising and you could hear the wind. People were screaming and I can still hear it. It was so frustrating we couldn't do anything to help. I'm a kind of a recluse and I don't go out and do neighborhood things. I knew everyone by sight and who lived where. I'd wave from the porch.

It was horrifying after the water was down but not gone. Our Biloxi fire fighters got me out of the attic. Bob had gotten down before. They took us over the rubble and the bodies of the people who didn't make it. Eighty percent who stayed didn't make it. There were 30 plus people in the mission on Howard Avenue and the people at the VFW who didn't make it and people in our neighborhood. They took us to the middle school on Irish Hill. There was no power, no water, and it was monitored by the police and fire department.

We were there two to three weeks. The day after the Red Cross got here, the shelter was closed due to dysentery. The National Guard was forcefully getting people to evacuate from the shelter.

I was visibly upset. Who would take care of the dogs? They were getting fed and watered. I went back Thursday after the storm. The dogs couldn't go to the shelter.

A young couple from Tampa went out and bought me two pair of shorts that would fit me and he let me use his cell phone. I got through to Thomas' voice mail. He was a volunteer firefighter and could get through checkpoints to get to us.

When we got here, to Saucier, there were nineteen people, some in tents. The shelter is a whole different nightmare: no supplies, no blankets. We looked after each other. It was very hot during the day so we'd sleep by the doors so we could be near any air coming in. They fed children first, then women, and anything left, we got. One night we had six Pringles and ketchup. We were grateful for it, that's what we were eating.

We were right behind the Methodist retreat. People from the neighborhood gave us food. One Red Cross local volunteer handled all the food for 1100 people. The hospital was overrun.

It was a nightmare like something out of a third world civil war, like a bomb had just gone off, like someone nuked us.

At the shelter a group formed in the hallway and we stuck up for each other and looked out for each other. We went out to the beach and scrounged clothes from the tourist shops. We found a few things like a stool to sit on. Little things were a big triumph.

God bless the police and firemen who lost everything. They were helping us. One officer in particular named Patrick took me to my house. He got a city vehicle and got my medicine and some things to wash out and check on the dogs.

I think it showed us how really unprepared this super power is for something like this to happen on our soil. They were no means ready for something of this magnitude. FEMA really dropped the ball on this one.

My family was frantically trying to find me but kept getting misdirected or misinformed or downright stonewalled! It wasn't until the last week we were there, in the shelter, when volunteer EMTs from Tampa took phone numbers and messages and radioed it to a dispatch in Tampa and relayed messages for us. That was the first time my family knew I was okay.

My doctor seems to think I had a TIA, small stroke, during the storm and I still have trouble sleeping. I was talking to a good friend of mine, a priest in Philadelphia, and he said, sure you have trouble sleeping-- you have PTSD (Post Traumatic Stress Disorder).

We've gotten some help from FEMA. We found a house to rent and are waiting for FEMA to come through with the first payment.

It's a pretty intense experience. I wouldn't wish it on anyone.

Musings

Before Katrina I had planned to go to Pema Chödrön's retreat/meditation in Colorado. I had heard she wasn't going to teach in 2006 and I felt this was my chance to hear her in person. I arrived in Colorado on Aug. 25th and watched the news on CNN and saw Katrina in Florida. They showed three possible paths she could take. I wasn't worried. I had sat on my front porch and watched Dennis, the hurricane before Katrina, bring a little bit of rain and wind for four hours and it was predicted to be serious. It was the first time in nine years I boarded up my windows. Everyone in the condos boarded up for Dennis. It was as if we were practicing for what was to come.

On Friday, Aug. 26th, I couldn't sleep at all. I thought it was because I was in a dorm with 12 people and some people snored. Unbeknownst to me, friends on the Coast were already boarding up and leaving.

I participated in 6:00 a.m. Yoga every morning during the retreat. On Monday morning, August 29th, the morning of the hurricane, I had cramps and a terribly upset stomach. I thought I was going to throw up. I thought maybe I was releasing some old stuff. Little did I know I was releasing all "my stuff" to the Gulf waters. I had never had that reaction to Yoga. The next morning I again didn't feel well during Yoga. When I got to Denver airport, Tuesday morning, Aug. 30th I saw the devastation in Biloxi on the news. I was shocked.

The retreat I attended was called *No Time To Lose*. It was the study of the chapter on patience in the *Way of the Bodhisattva* by Shantideva. How appropriate given what was to come. A fascinating story occurred during the workshop.

> It was Monday and many of the 400 participants were enthralled with the bookstore, a chance to get many treasures. I was coming up the path from the meditation tent and I met a woman who had just come from the bookstore and she relayed this story. She was in line

with many books and other objects of adoration when she bumped into the woman in front of her who had a soda and it spilled all over the woman's books. And the woman's reply to the woman who bumped into her was, "Thank you for clearing the karma between us in one shot." The woman who caused the soda to spill asked if she could replace the books and the woman said no she did not want any karma left. This woman had beautifully put the teachings we had just learned to practice.

"Safe Harbor in the Storm"

Jayson Sutkus and Leslie Wilder live in Ocean Springs, Mississippi. Jayson came from New York to New Orleans, then Lafayette, Louisiana and in 1978 he came to the MS Gulf Coast. Leslie was born in Memphis and then came to the Coast from Starkville, Mississippi in 1989. Jayson created Ascension Reiki and Leslie, a yoga teacher, has helped him expand the process. They do Ascension Reiki attunements for people around the world.

At 7:00 a.m. we started out playful and inquisitive and we knew it was a storm. We walked into the back yard and down to the marsh and small bayou where the water was beginning to rise. We had a porch swing way down in that area and as we sat in the rain on the porch swing, the water just touched our toes. Realizing that we really weren't in a safe place, we moved up the hill to a more sturdy tree. We decided to play a game of moving a brick to a mark where the water would stop rising. Jayson had a brick and I had another. We marked our places on the ground and said, "Okay, the water is not going to move beyond this brick." Ten minutes would pass and then we would move the brick again and again and again. While we were standing by the oak in the bayou, we witnessed the water moving the earth. There was actually a pulse of the ocean that was flowing from beneath, causing the earth to swell, rise, and fall. As we held the tree we could feel the wind shaking its inner core. Never before have we felt such sensations.

There are three huge Magnolias that guard the back side of our property line in the bayou area. Knowing that they were stronger than the rest of the trees, we stood by them for the longest time watching the water rise up to our feet. Yes, by that time it had risen above the line of Hurricane Camille.

We discovered at that time that the water was already getting into our neighbor's home, so Jayson and I started back to the house to get our wallets and our cell phones. By the time we got out of the house the water was up to the calves of our legs and when we got out of the house, we couldn't shut the door because of all the water, mud, leaves, and debris that was being heaved into our home. I remember watching the water as if it was heaving and throwing up into my house. I remember saying in my mind, "It's okay...It's okay," connecting with the water as if it was a living entity and trying to calm it down.

We couldn't shut the door! No matter how hard we tried. Jayson said, "Just leave it...Leave it alone, Leslie." My hand was on the doorknob. I remember pausing and then letting go of everything I ever owned. Geared up in the survival mode, Jayson grabbed a ladder and said, "Come on, let's get on the roof."

I went into a state of shock, overwhelmed with what I saw. There was no way with Jayson sitting behind me (even with his arms around me and wrapping a yellow raincoat around me) that I could stay warm. I was shivering, not by the cold, but by nerves. I was shaking. We were numbed to the sound all around us. I remember saying to Jayson, "In the distance I hear boom, boom." We thought something really happened there. No trees were falling, few limbs, nothing to make us believe that we were in the worst disaster to hit the US. The only thing that made us feel it was bad was the water kept coming up like a toilet overflowing. "Make it stop." We were watching across the bayou and said, "Did it get into their house yet?" Little knowing it was coming into our house.

As we sat there we saw little wisps of wind tornadoes racing down the rising flood waters. We watched our cars in the front of the house swimming around with the pulse of the water, the constant rising and falling of the Mother of Waters. Keeping our eyes on little watermarks, we could tell the water was beginning to recede. An armadillo came swimming by the side of our house looking for shelter as we sat huddled on the roof until a neighbor, who had not been as flooded, saw us and decided that we were not safe and needed to get off.

He took us to his house which was only a few doors down, and there we stayed for about an hour until the water receded enough for us to get back home. While we were gone from our home, there was a huge longleaf pine in our neighbor's yard that fell. At that time, many limbs in the Magnolias snapped and were twisted. It seems to me that the damage to the back yard occurred when we were not present. Could it have been that we were actually being guardians of our own yard, or was it that the angels wanted us to get off the roof because they knew we were not going to be safe in the next hour?

When we got back to our home, we found everything that was below our knees soaked and stained with mud, leaves, water and debris. We quickly grabbed our rakes and shovels and started moving the mess out. Oh yes, it was not only mud but the sewer lines had backed up and flowed into the house as well.

Every piece of furniture that we owned was moved somewhere that day to start the cleaning process. Some pieces were taken outside to dry while others were too big to move. The mattress and box springs were the first to go into what we were to know for the next 12 days as The Pile. It was by the side of the street in our front yard, which eventually grew into a mountain range that lined both sides of Evelyn Drive's neighborhood. Books, major appliances, my computer and many other modern day conveniences like our two cars were damaged beyond repair from the storm.

Jayson: The shock of our life came after we finished clearing out all the debris from the house and then walked to the beach. I was laughing and crying at the same time. Broken water pipes spewing fountains, houses slid into the bayou and other houses totally gone. Leslie said, "The bulldozers were really working hard today." Just slabs, no houses at the beach. Some were standing and gutted and here we are playing with bricks and seeing the water as a toilet.

Jayson: It was weird when up on the roof the armadillo swims by, and we saw fences swaying, rippling and floating, attached to the bottom somehow. The ground was heaving, I was standing on it and it came up about a foot. You could see it moving, the roots moving, the trees swaying you could see or feel this from inside.

Leslie: The most interesting thing about the storm was to observe how the water penetrated the ground. This tidal surge was not just on the surface of the ground, it was covering and totally saturated the earth. We were on the earth and felt the water's waves. We could feel the motion of the water swell and we were standing on the ground. There was a giving and receding and that is why the water was penetrating and eating the earth under the trees.

Jayson: The ground was moving. The first time I felt it I thought I was hallucinating.

Leslie: The water had risen that high (into our yard) and everything was in constant motion. Everything was moving. You would get a shaking of the trees from the wind, then the swell of the ocean inside the earth.

Jayson: The incredible thing was the gust of winds that lasted four to five minutes sweeping down the bayou. You could see tornadoes and water spouts. The marsh became a bayou, then a lake, then waterfront property.

Leslie: I learned as Jayson and I were playing with the mode of innocence with angels that they alone were protecting us. During the storm I did not know this.

Jayson: We had a safe harbor in the storm, like we were in a bubble.

We were not ever afraid. Now we know more than ever before we were safe and protected and allowed to witness not knowing. The pain has come from seeing the devastation and not being able to understand being so close and not knowing. Two people were killed up the street. The water came up and swept them out of the house.

Just three houses away there was a huge pine tree that crashed into a neighbor's bedroom where she was sleeping. It broke the back side of the house out and she was swept out on the mattress. Every house from here over was not livable, just a lot of destruction.

We were the first that were saved, spared. We had a few shingles gone and water in the house. We had mainly work, but we didn't have to move anywhere. We slept on a wet floor for a couple of days.

The first night there was dead silence. Stars were so bright and we had fires every night. One night we played our didgeridoo and someone was playing a flute and we were communicating like Indians.

Leslie: Another thing I found out about my family, closest of kin, was that they were the ones who reached out and supported me. Mom and Dad called every other day. I hadn't talked to my Dad for seven years. And I know who my friends really are and the ones who are not. Certain friends would give their life to make sure we were okay.

Tanis brought us gasoline, food, and money. She packed up herself and stuff and came down here from Jackson. She was the first one and she came three weekends in a row. She wanted to help, do anything she could.

This is a personal time for me. I was given the name "Spirits Wind" at least a year ago by the Masters. The reason I was given it was because I didn't like my name Leslie. This was given because they told me that is what my name means to them. It's the lee side. The lee is the calm side of the wind, the calm side of self. It is the side not afraid to stand in the wind, the side that steps outside of self, doesn't hide behind an island. When you are egoless, you are in spirit.

Jayson: "The Winds" lee side is the side that is not the direct side of the wind. It is shielded by the wind so you can stand in the wind because you are sheltered. We were in the calm of the storm, we stood on the lee side of the trees.

I learned about how important family and friends are and people in the neighborhood. We got to know our neighbors and everyone helped each other and that was good.

How I changed, my consciousness shifted. We're in slow motion. We're in a different time frame. Before the storm we had a schedule. Since the storm schedules never happen in the time frame you plan. Some event happens to change the plan and time frame. There is always something. You learn to go with the flow. Your ideas of what needs to get done are more of a direction than actual sequence of events.

Leslie: We moved but we did not go anywhere. It has taken us months to see how we fit in. We can now see the water from our house because parts of other houses are gone and many tree limbs are down.

Musings

There are these mysteries in life that we do not understand. We cannot get our minds around them. The most fascinating part of the process is that it is out of our minds. It is beyond the logical. These are the real everyday realities, the ones we cannot explain. They seem to be happening more and more often. The flow seems to be occurring more often and our brain is beginning to function as it was meant to function, as a hologram. An example is the reflexes in the body. In the study of reflexology, we find there are reflexes in our feet that correspond to different organs and body parts. When a reflexologist presses on these points i.e., the reflex for the back, the back is then stimulated and the pain that was there will subside. These reflexes are also in the hands and our ears. In Iridology the iris is the reflex that shows what is going on in the rest of our body. My friend Betty Sue O'Brian, a diplomat in Iridology instruction, calls it God's MRI.

The idea that parts of our body contain the whole of the body is the example of the hologram. In the hologram every part contains the whole. Holograms are not all that solid, just as we are not all solid. If we look at subatomic particles we see there are waves and particles and neither one is solid. In fact we only see the particles when we observe them. We are more fluid than we would like to imagine.

In meditation and prayer you can move from this three-dimensional physical reality to other realities. When people talk about miracles they are describing things happening beyond our ordinary everyday reality.

If this is so and there are many more dimensions than the third dimension we normally observe, we are perhaps in for a global shift in consciousness that lets us move between dimensions. Maybe Katrina shifted some people and some things into other dimensions during the storm.

To give an example of the miracles that can happen when shifting dimensions, I offer the following story a friend of mine told me several years ago.

> Her daughter was going blind and she had taken her to every eye specialist she could find, and her daughter did not get better. Then she took her to an alternative medicine practitioner and was given some things to do. Her daughter's eyes got better. This friend of mine was so happy and grateful that she was in this high state of gratitude as she approached Highway 29 to go home. What she did not realize was that she was going in the wrong direction into the oncoming traffic. Before she knew it she was passing THROUGH a truck coming right at her from the other direction with the driver in awe as she waved to him. This experience she credits to her high state of gratefulness.

This is only one story of many of my friends who have passed through so-called solid objects without any problem. We are much more than our physical bodies.

The most interesting phenomena are of course in the new places, the places where the rules do not work--not the places where they do work! That is the way in which we discover new rules.

--Richard Feynman, Physicist, Nobel Laureate

If we could see this world as more illusion than real we might suffer less. Letting go of fear, can we see things as a child with a sense of wonder? This wonder gives us an opportunity to let go and lighten up. If we can become this "Child of Illusion," as Pema Chödrön describes, "We become mindful, awake, and gentle with our hopes and fears. We see them clearly with less bias, less judgement and less sense of a heavy trip. Finding that soft tender part that is within ourselves as we open our hearts more and more helps us get to this place."

"Understanding What Drives People to Extremes"

Carroll Campbell grew up on the coast in Ocean Springs, Mississippi. She lived in Maryland for four years and spent one year in Wales during college. She works for Catholic charities.

I decided to stay because my parents decided to stay. My parents decided to stay because my aunt wanted to stay. I heard on NPR (National Public Radio) that it was a Category 5 with a 30 foot storm surge on Saturday morning. I said, "Mom, we need to go." Mom believed if my aunt's house was okay in Camille it would be okay. One year ago a Category 5 hurricane was predicted and my aunt thought it was ridiculous to leave then.

Mom had a house in Wiggins we could have gone to. My aunt refused to go this time also. I wouldn't have stayed with my aunt; I would have gone with my parents. They are disabled. I kept asking how high my aunt's house was on Howard Avenue (very close to the Point). Our story is not as dramatic as others.

Monday morning we got up at 7:00-7:30 a.m. We had five people in the house: my mother, Clara; Aunt Helen; stepfather, Sylvester; sister, Abbey; myself; and one dog and seven cats.

It was blowing and raining. We were cooking breakfast. At 8:45 a.m. I saw water in the backyard and thought it was strange. I saw water in front of Howard Ave. I kept walking back and forth and said, "It is starting to fill up our cars." It was high enough to reach the porch, which was 3 feet off the ground. We still were very quiet. I was concerned but not hysterical.

So the water started coming in the middle of the house, seeping up through the floor, through the lowest point of this 100 year old house. Then it started coming in the doors. We began to eat very fast. I went to the bathroom because I knew I might not be able to go later. I put my contacts in and my tennis shoes on so I wouldn't cut my feet.

My dad put floatation devices on himself, Mom, and my sister (who is 25 and mentally disabled), and my aunt. I didn't have one but I could swim and felt confident about that.

My aunt started to collect the animals. She didn't have a plan to get them. She was putting the cats in the cages together and I thought that was crazy because we needed to save the people first but I didn't say anything.

So my dad suggested we go into the attic. I was trying to figure out how we could get there. We had a wooden ladder. My aunt and I could swim and I felt we could pull everyone else up. We set the ladder up and realized it wasn't tall enough and realized it would float when the water reached a certain height. We were talking about the ladder and my Aunt said there was a metal one in the garage. The water was slowly climbing. In some places it was 1 1/2 feet. It was surreal, because a house is supposed to protect you from nature. This was the real experience and it was very moving and very disturbing.

We had to get the ladder and we went into the backyard and walked into the water. Luckily the house was surrounded by chicken wire and it kept the debris away. The water didn't hit as strong as it did on the beach. We had several houses buffering us.

So when we went out in the yard the water was chest high. I am thinking,"Yuk!" It was moving and swirling around me. So we opened the garage and got the ladder and carried it back into the house. The whole time I wasn't panicking, but thought, "If this gets higher, we could die." I was thinking, "We need to do something, what are our options? Do we stay inside, go outside, can we just float up with water, what are the exits, what are the outs?"

My mom and dad were sitting because they are disabled and we had to stay very present, one moment at a time. So the discussion between me, my dad and aunt was what was the next best thing to do?

So we got the ladder set up. Then my dad said, "We need food and water up there." So that is what we did next. We carried up food and water. After that the dog food. Around that time my aunt carried things to the ladder and I pulled it up. We had an axe and crowbar in case we needed to get through the roof.

At that point we had everything in the attic and my dad said, "I think the water has stopped rising." I said, "Let's wait a few minutes to see if it starts rising again." So we waited 20 minutes and my dad said, "I think its going down now." And I came down out of the attic. I said, "Let's leave stuff up there in case it starts rising again." I didn't trust it wasn't going to start rising again.

Finally it receded substantially and the wind and rain were still blowing. So in the course of two hours it went down and down, and all I could do was think how relieved I was and so thankful. My aunt got very concerned about the floors and mud. The water in the house was between one and one and one-half feet. The house has different levels.

At one point I saw our cars floating outside and my dad said they were doing a "dance in the road." Finally the water went down on Howard Avenue and there was all this debris. My mom said, "Where did all that come from?" And I said, "Maybe a house collapsed." I think we then ate something. Then around 2:00-3:00 p.m. we started seeing police and rescue people. I opened the back door and saw a fireman and he asked, "Are you okay? "I said, "We are fine." They were looking around to see how everyone was and I was glad to see them.

I started to help my aunt clean the mud off the floor and that's all I did was scrape mud. We only had a little water so there wasn't much we could do. So around mid-afternoon a policeman and policewoman drove by and mom said "stop them," I want to talk to them.

A neighbor came over before the police came. She was hysterical and very emotional and shared with us that all the debris was the houses on the beach. "All the houses on the beach are gone." I didn't believe it. Mom stopped these cops and asked the woman, "Do you have any information about Porter Avenue by the lighthouse?" The policewoman said,"Yes Ma' am, all those beautiful houses are gone." She had to say it three times for my mom to get it. I still didn't believe it, and I said, "That means my house is gone, my cats are dead." And at that point my aunt hugged me. So the first thing (it is funny) I thought about was my cats and then my favorite pair of red high heel shoes. "They're gone." I kept saying things like how could they ALL be gone. They were incredibly well-built houses, built for hurricanes, and I'm very skeptical anyway. I don't believe what people tell me even if I read it in the paper.

I kept saying, "I need to go see my house." But it was impossible because of the debris and wind. The wind blew for hours and hours. We kept saying to ourselves, "I can't believe it is still blowing!" It kept up until 5:00 or 6:00 p.m.

My aunt and I walked about one block with the dog. We walked down as far as Keller, one and one half blocks. We tried to see but there was too much debris. It was difficult to see. Before we walked, I saw one of my best friends, Lee, who lived on Keller and asked, "Are you okay?" She said, "Yes but my house is gone. I just spent three hours on my neighbor's roof." I wanted to invite her in but there were tensions in the family already so I felt I couldn't do it.

People kept coming from The Point and were carrying food. Really small children were walking. They were all a mess. I'm sure they were all in flooded-out houses. I had been lucky at this point, and I didn't know how much flooding there had been. They were wet, dirty and everyone was a mess. They were going to the community center. I went by later and lots and lots of people were outside but there didn't seem to be any plan.

The next morning my dad and I hitched a ride to Dad's house from a nurse from Biloxi Regional who worked in the baby unit there. He was pretty strung out and he had his concerns. He had things on his mind, his family. He drove us down there to Porter Avenue and he waited while we walked. Even though my dad doesn't move fast, he has a bad back and bad hips. From the back his house looked okay, but it was piled with debris. BP was gone, Bulton's Pawn Shop, Russene's Antiques was demolished, Moran's Art Studio was gone.

Then we came around front and I saw the bottom floor was gutted and I walked up to it and started calling my mom's cats. I don't think we went to my house then because my dad couldn't walk much farther. We went up to the house and found one cat; it came up from downstairs. The front wall was gone and we could see downstairs. I called "kitty, kitty" and she came and I picked her up. I knew my mom was going to be overjoyed to see her. Dad and I went back to the guy's car, and he drove us back to Howard Avenue and we told my mom what happened. She was glad to get the cat and I said that the bottom floor was washed out. It had antiques, crystal, china. But upstairs had been fine, you would never know a storm had come through. I didn't get to see my house until the day after. I walked. It is about a 30 minute walk. It was on the beach and it was fine and my pets were fine. It was a miracle. It was buffered by other homes around me. Salt water came up high enough to soak and kill the house plants on the porch. And this property is the highest property in this area--the highest, if not the highest in Biloxi, according to my grandfather. Supposedly my house was 50 feet above sea level; it is very high. It is next to the cemetery. My mom's grandmother built this house. My mother's home was 22 feet above sea level. The water seeped under the front door and wet the carpet there. It came under the front bedroom window enough to bring in some silt. It must have then receded. And that was it. And that's all I've had, a little silt and dead plants. I'm incredibly lucky.

I was really bothered by the fact that there were not enough hurricane shelters. The school across the street from us is two story and could have been used. It could have protected people but it wasn't used. The civil defense needs to do a better job of setting up hurricane shelters. If you had money you could leave; however, many didn't and couldn't and did not have any place to go. It is one thing to choose to stay and take a risk, but it's another to be too poor to go. Civil defense needed to do more.

There was nothing on WLOX (local TV) that I know of in Spanish or Vietnamese to warn people of the magnitude of the storm. They still treat them like they are not here. It is appalling. This is a diverse area. Some Mexicans died in a set of apartments on Irish Hill. I heard people died there that were Mexican and didn't get the word. This is hearsay, but I saw a lot of Mexican people walking around after the storm.

This made this an exciting place to be before the storm. The ethnic diversity. And WLOX and *The Sun Herald*, except for human interest stories, do nothing to reach out. Even though WLOX has a Vietnamese reporter, to the best of my knowledge no broadcast was done in Vietnamese.

Other than that the media did a good job. They did announce the storm surge and evacuation plans. Mississippi Public Broadcast (MPB), was announcing the danger of the storm surge and did a pretty good job after the storm of telling about the distribution centers. It took about three days to start these up.

Unfortunately, I couldn't hear the radio in the house because my aunt was too freaked out, though it was very comforting for me to hear them. It was a familiar voice and lifeline. We really depended on

WLOX. They were really troopers and hung in there. Because of them we have all that documentation and information for the Attorney General lawsuit and it took a lot of guts.

Personally you learn what you are capable of handling during extreme stress. You learn what your limits are. The worst parts of your personality and best come through. I lost my temper some days and wondered why I couldn't be calmer. Extreme stress gives you a short fuse. As human beings, we can't handle extreme stress without reacting. No one can be a saint through extreme stress. I got an inkling why people beat their kids. They are so strung out and lose control. You understand what drives people to extremes.

I really appreciated my family in a whole new way. I lived with my stepsister for six weeks. My mom and sister weren't getting along. I don't know what we would have done without my stepsister Rose.

Musings

Thich Nhat Hanh, when writing about mothers, says, *"mother" cannot be separated from that of "love". He recalls the following poem he heard as a child.*

That year, although I was still very
young
my mother left me,
and I realized that I was an orphan,

everyone around me was crying,
I suffered in silence...
Allowing the tears to flow,
I felt my pain soften.

Evening enveloped
Mother's tomb,
the pagoda bell rang sweetly.
I realized that to lose your mother
is to lose the whole universe.

"Every day we do things, we are things that have to do with peace,

if we are aware of our life...., our way of looking at things,

we will know how to make peace right in the moment, we are alive. "

--Thich Nhat Hahn

Sacred Pathways, Apr/May 2004, Vol. 7 No 2, Thich Nhat Hahn, *A rose for your pocket. pg. 18*

"Hurricane Tales"

A story was sent to me via email by a person who felt it needed to be told but did not have the permission of the author, so it will be told anonymously.

Before the storm I called my friend, Jay, a bridge buddy, to invite him to weather the storm together as we had done before. I cooked a nice dinner of bacon-wrapped steaks, asparagus, and salad. Our first problem arose when the electricity went out--the battery-operated TV had plenty of cells, but the wrong size. Fortunately I had purchased a radio from a credit card offer that had two weather stations on it. We checked the best place to put Jay's car Sunday night. Sunday morning fancy cooking was OUT, but we had plenty of food from the fridge. I had also stocked several cases of bottled water.

We watched as the storm took all the leaves off my beautiful magnolia, but suddenly we were surrounded by water and it rose rapidly. The front door broke and at first we tried to bail out the water...futile. I put the leashes on the dogs; we got the stairway to the attic down, but somehow I got caught between the kitchen door and its frame by rising water. Jay had a tough time freeing me. Alfie and Annie, the toy poodles, reached into their gene pool and did a perfect dog paddle. They were resistant to the attic stairs but we got them up there. Couldn't see anything of our surroundings, but Jay did see the cat, Kitty, float by on a pillow and into my bedroom. We watched the water climb up the stairs, and we had eleven rungs free when it stopped. After an indeterminate period the water began to recede slowly and finally out of the house, leaving sopping wet carpet and furniture in a prone position. We couldn't get the door to my bedroom open, but we could hear Kitty meowing.

Fortunately, a strong Biloxi policeman came by the next day and put his shoulder to the bedroom door. Kitty was atop my bed, clearly saying, "What took you so long?" The oxygen company had left a four day supply of O₂ that did not require electricity. One day firemen came through looking for bodies. None in our area, really high ground. We found Jay's car across the street about six houses down the road away from the Gulf. We made arrangements for my handyman to take care of the roof leaks. Someone's house was in my front yard and four lovely desk chairs from the Merrill Lynch building on the Gulf were in the back yard, along with a kitchen cabinet drawer of the highest quality. My neighbor's house had lost the center section and a small house was caught in the branches of a huge oak in the small park in front of my house. Rubble was everywhere.

I guess it was Tuesday that I woke up and heard someone calling my name, asking if I were in the house. It was the head of Home Instead, a franchise agency for the care of older patients. I had used their services extensively after leaving the hospital the second time in 2005. His people were coming in five days a week for five hours before the storm. He insisted Jay and I come to his home where there was RUNNING WATER. His home was in Ocean Springs on a high bluff, quite a way from the Gulf. His neighbors were cooking up their freezer contents so we had nice hot meals. After the first night we went back to my house to pick up the dogs. Started up my car in the garage, new Ford Crown Vic, which had been blown so hard that it broke the garage doors open. Took Alfie and Annie out to the Whispering Pines Doggie Dude Ranch. Miss Wanda had had some dogs picked up by their owners so she could take others in. They know her well, and certainly looked like refugees. The car made it over to Jay's house in Ocean Springs, where it died and could not be restarted. I left Kitty with the house; his regular cat sitter was prepared to help him. He grew up feral and I felt he would not be relocated easily.

Jay's office got electricity and phone service, so he called our families and made arrangements to get us out of there. He did get a chance to see where his apartment had been, now obliterated. His family in Connecticut bought him a ticket and hired a taxi to go from Mobile to Ocean Springs, where it picked him up and brought him to the airport. Meanwhile, my St. Louis family was arguing with the highway patrol who maintained that no one could get south within 200 miles of Biloxi. My nephew and great-nephew went to Nashville and dropped South from there to Mobile and Ocean Springs, buying gas in containers all the way. With their provisions we went due North and could finally get gas in Missouri. We arrived at 2:30 a.m. Sunday and my clever Sarah had oxygen waiting for me. She is office manager in a physicians' office, so I have a team of experts on my side. I wonder where my "main man" is.

Life has really been cushy here. My friend Carol got back from Atlanta and has electricity and water (non-potable). She lives a block from me. No one in her huge family was a casualty, but many lost homes. True of many of my friends. I know some of them are safe, and we talk as often as we can.

2005 has not been a good year for me! Thank you all for your interest and affection.

Musings

"I can be changed by what happens to me

But I refuse to be reduced by it."

--Maya Angelou

"When I grow up I am going to wear purple"

What sustains us, what keeps us going?

"Feeling a Sense of Healing"

Brian Murphy came to the Coast from Toronto in December 2004. He had been in Toronto for 5 years. Brian is originally from Indianapolis.

During the storm, I was going to be at home in North Biloxi, Popps Ferry Road. A friend said come over to Lee's house for a hurricane party in D'Iberville behind the post office.

Sunday around 6:00-6:30 p.m. I went over and we were all there, eight adults, ages 24-43, all males and four dogs and three cats. During the evening we watched TV and played board games. We had the weather channel on and watched the first news reports.

I remember the storm started early on Sunday. The rain started about 10:30 p.m. and the winds were picking up. While in the kitchen I remember the garage door was getting torn off its frame. I remember the power went out about 1:30 p.m. on Monday and we mostly got candles and a battery to operate the lights. We were all in the living room and wondering if the window would blow in. We moved forward to see out and then moved away because of the wind and the possibility of it blowing in.

I remember sitting in the living room on the end of the coach with my back to the front window and everybody kept saying, "Everyone stay away from the window." We saw the water come up the street. Then it was a foot deep and the storm drains were flooded. The window then was smashed by a 2 x 4 and the glass exploded into the house. The water was halfway up the street and someone said "it is flooded." Lee, the owner, said "We aren't in a flood plane. It isn't flooding." Then the water was up to the house but not inside.

I went and got two closet doors and put them over the window and got 2 x 4's out of the garage and nailed them in place. By then the water was in the back of the house and we were watching it come higher and higher but still not in the house. Then it began coming in the front door and we went to get bags of topsoil and potting soil and put them in front of the door like sand bags. The wind was blowing really strong at that point. The way we put the door on the window, only the bottom pane blew in on the window.

The garage door started blowing in and the whole door with the frame. Then we watched the water in back of the house getting deeper and deeper; it looked like an aquarium. It wasn't in the house yet. Then all of a sudden the living room started flooding, then the dinning room, and water was coming out of electrical sockets. After the water got to be 18 inches deep we decided to evacuate. We wondered where to go. All of the houses were one story, except the house next door was a two story. Something floated up to the front yard; it was bright yellow and we thought it was construction equipment. It was a row boat upside down. The neighbor next door grabbed the boat and put his wife and children in it and started heading toward the second story house. On this street of 35-45 houses, 10-12 houses had people in them. The only other two story was at the end of the street. The radio said, "Don't go outside."

At first we thought we could go into the attic. The radio said, "Don't go into the attic unless you have an axe to chop your way out." I thought we'd go to the house next door. No one was home. We'd have to break in. The neighbors from the other side in the boat were already there and smashed in the patio doors. We all went next door and went upstairs. Already 2 other families were there, the one next to Lee's house and the one across the street and us, 17 people. We were in the master bedroom on the second floor, a Korean family was in the little girl's room and in another room, the office had an Asian family. All in all, from the time the water started coming in and then going out seemed like two hours, but it was 45 minutes. The water crested at three and one-half to four feet.

When the water went out, we surveyed the damage in Lee's house and worked on getting the kitchen and dining room out, pulling the carpet and padding up. We had a barbecue grill to cook on and we cooked the meat in the freezer before it went bad. We stayed that night because everyone's car was flooded out. The next day my friend Eric found people he knew with a truck and they took me to my house.

Pine trees were down everywhere and I thought the house was probably smashed. I was on three acres with lots of pine trees. There were pine trees down across the driveway and we made our way to the house. Debris was everywhere. The house appeared fine with no damage I could see, except the chimney cap was gone.

I got the car out of the garage and I couldn't get out because of the trees from the trailer park next door. My neighbor has heavy equipment. He has a swimming pool business, and he cleared the driveway in 20 minutes. When I got out I went on to Lee's house and I had only a half tank of gas, so the first thing I did was take everyone to check on their homes and families and friends that were close by.

Everyone's home was fine except Chris was on the beach and it was just a slab. I went out for supplies to Wal-mart. The line was already around the back of the building. I went to Winn Dixie and it wasn't open but had trucks full of ice. I got ice and then it was getting dark. The curfew was 6:00 p.m. We all went back to my house and it was high and dry. We hung out, played board games and dice and hung out on the patio. It was very hot.

The next morning I got up and had breakfast. My house was on a well but I didn't have well power. I had a camp stove for cooking and had $200 in food supplies. I had twelve gallons of bottled water; I had filled the tub so it was full of water and I had a rain barrel full of water.

I used the rain barrel to flush the toilet. I used the tub to bathe in after eight very dirty people used it. It took a week to get all the dirt out.

Then trying to find gas stations that were open was difficult. The ones open had tremendous lines. There were no food distribution centers yet.

The next night my friend Eric was in my house and everyone else went back to Lee's. The day after that I heard about looting, shooting at helicopters and Red Cross trucks being hijacked on the radio. I didn't know the location of the station that was reporting, whether it was Alabama or New Orleans. There were so many rumors spreading. I heard that Treasure Bay (a casino shaped like a pirate ship) was in the mall parking lot and it had its nose into shore.

When we heard all the stories we felt things were going to get a lot worse before getting better. That was before anyone thought about leaving. When we heard the stories and things were getting crazier my friend Eric and I left for Indianapolis at 4:00 p.m. that afternoon.

We were on mental overdrive. There was no time to think and absorb it. Never did we feel scared or feared for our lives; everyone stayed calm. It was more like a feeling of adventure. During it there was a peace and calm, take it as it comes, do what we can.

That morning we left was Saturday and I was down and had a good hard cry. It was overwhelming sadness for all of those who lost so much and I only lost my car.

After we left we came back four days later. The whole time I was gone I couldn't wait to come back. I wanted to help, I wanted to stay but felt since I had the means to leave, I would be a drain on the resources.

I didn't know how long before the banks and ATM's would be up. I only had $200 in cash. I didn't get home until 12:30 at night. There were two cars in my driveway. I thought they were squatters but it was my neighbors.

We had no water, no electricity. I was able to go to the back of the property to the city water and run a hose to the back of the house. The gas was on and the cable was still out. I went around to my friends to check on them. With all the extent of the damage I never got to see the beach. I still haven't been to the beach. I've only been one block from it.

What made me decide to stay was even though I haven't lived here a long time, this is my home. When I came down to Mississippi I thought I'd only stay for the winter. But I found I was unconditionally loved and accepted. I felt this is where I belong and need to be. I felt called to stay here even after the storm. I feel this is where I need to be. I was sticking with my life plan by staying. After the winter, I kind of felt like I had decided to stay and I had lots of lessons to learn from Katrina. The lessons kept me here before and after the storm. I've got a lot of learning and healing to do. Everyone comes to the Coast and feels a sense of healing. Now after the storm I realize it has helped me in my healing and I can help others.

As far as what I've learned from it... there really isn't anything I can't handle. Trial by fire and I came out without being burned. There are a lot of lessons there to be learned, not to get stuck in material things. I already knew that. When I lost my car, I didn't really care because I could get a new one.

Musings

Healing comes in many forms, and if we are open to it, there is a tremendous gift from the process. It is not an event that all of a sudden happens and we are "Healed." Most of the time it is a gradual unfolding of ourselves that we allow to happen with conscious intent. As in an evolutionary leap, all of a sudden we know we are different. We begin to notice our behavior has changed. We begin to feel our depths more. Things that were so important to us seem to be forgotten.

Some people say, "I feel whole again." Many begin to see how we are more alike than different from one another. If we were to put it on a bumper sticker, it might say, "I have arrived!" Or it can be very unassuming. Sometimes in the quiet of the moment more can be done than in any string of words.

When AIDS began to spread silently to a wider population the common denominator was compassion for all, no matter what one's lifestyle.

Riding through New Jersey last year on my way home to Mississippi I was listening to station WBAI out of New York. It is part of the Pacifica Broadcasting Company. There was a doctor on the show Majid Ali, MD talking about prostate cancer. He has treated many patients with both traditional and nontraditional treatments. One of the stories was of a man who went the non-traditional route for prostrate cancer and got well. A caller asked if the doctor would recommend alternative or nontraditional treatment to his patients. His answer was, "No!" When asked why, his reply was, "Some people get well with traditional treatment and others with non-traditional." If a patient comes to him and says they believe or want to use nontraditional treatment he is supportive of their journey and wishes. The bottom line according to Dr. Ali is not the treatment that you use but the patient's remembrance of their divinity. His belief is in the person's conscious awareness of the divinity within and how that makes a difference in the healing process. We are divine beings greater than we can imagine. To believe our divinity is to become whole.

"A Lot More Respect for Mother Nature"

Ben Richards is 19 years old and was born in Memphis, Tennessee. He has lived in his home in Long Beach, Mississippi since he was six years old.

We started boarding up the day before and the police came by saying there is a mandatory evacuation and they couldn't help us during the storm. My dad works for Coast Electric and he had to stay. I have two younger brothers and they went to Atlanta with my grandma. I was supposed to leave with my fiancé to go to Tunica, Mississippi and found out my dad was staying by himself. I couldn't leave my dad by himself in case something went wrong. So I decided to stay.

So we boarded up all the windows and got ready for the storm the day before. We didn't think it would be too bad. We've been here through a couple of hurricanes.

The next night we go to sleep like normal and then we woke up about 5:00 a.m. to see what the storm was doing. It was hazy outside and we had everything boarded up so we had to look under what was boarded up. I had to lay on my stomach to see out. So we are looking out the front door and the trees are flying.

My dad wakes me up. I went to sleep for 30 minutes, and I have never seen anything like it. The trees--75% were down everywhere and the water was coming up about three feet up to the house in front of us. Then about halfway in the front yard about one foot deep and then up the stairs. Then we came out to see if we're okay and how high it is.

Thirty minutes after that we could see it coming through the door and see water on the carpet. You could step on the carpet and it was bubbling up and it splashing as you stepped. It wasn't high yet. About fifteen minutes after that it was knee-deep. When you get 15 inches in the house you get furniture floating. The refrigerator went over and the garbage tipped over and was floating.

We were pacing from the front door to the back room because the house was on blocks and we were wondering if it would float us or fall down on top of us and if so we wouldn't survive. So we are walking back and forth and the water is getting higher all the time. It's knee deep, then waist deep and we are wondering what to do. My father wanted to jump out of the back window. This back room is full of windows and we had two or three snakes trying to get in. The snakes were on the windows.

If it's waist deep inside it's chest deep outside. The house is one and one-half feet high in the back and two feet in front. We scrounged through all the stuff to find a rope and we tied ourselves together and got a baseball bat. I was on the phone the whole time with my fiancé. Her father suggested to get a rope and tie ourselves together. He also said to go to the attic and bring something to break through the roof.

By this time the winds are blowing 125-130 mph. This is the peak of the storm and we are still walking back and forth from the front of the house to the back room. So we look out and a piece of boardwalk from the beach was at the front door trying to break it and several 30 foot boats were bobbing like corks in the front yard. I never thought I'd see anything like this in my lifetime.

We decided to go into the attic. We marked how high the water was at 10:00 a.m. and another line for when it peaked. We had to either go in the attic or we would have to get out of the house. We do not stay too long (20 min.); we were so anxious the house would come down. The power was out and we could not see anything. The most depressing thing is the last time I talked to my fiancé (who is carrying our child), I am in the attic and the phone cuts out. That is the last time she hears from me for three days. She thought I was dead.

So we get down from the attic and there is a little current and the water is going out slowly and we are thanking God. It drops about a foot or so and as quick as it went down, it came back in like tidal waves. As if waves were sucking it out and pushing it back in.

It happened three or four times in about 45 minutes. Later it started going down and it stayed down. We were down here on the first floor as it came in and out. That was the most scary thing. If the house was to come off its blocks this is when it would do it. It didn't move off its blocks. The house was here before Camille; it was probably built in the 50's.

We came downstairs because I at least wanted to know what was going on. Life goes on.

The water eventually left and we went to my grandma who lives a half-block away. It took up to 30 minutes to walk half a block. We had to go over refrigerators, roofs, boats, trees, and whole houses. We got there and stayed put for awhile until my father's friend came and checked on us to see if we were alright. We stayed with him for three to four days in North Island View, north of the tracks. He had hot water and that was a blessing. I worked a couple of days and cleared a couple of lots and then went to California.

I know I learned one thing. If it's a Category 1 or 4 hurricane I'm not going to stay. Too much can happen. Grab what you can and leave.

I now do not doubt Mother Nature. If it's your time to go it's your time to go. I have a lot more respect for Mother Nature.

Musings

For all the fuss about the storm we seem to be finding out that there is a lot more learning and healing since the storm than there was before it. Katrina may have done the cleansing that was mentioned earlier on many levels. A nineteen year old staying for a Category 5 hurricane because he thinks more of his dad than the life threatening situation might help others look at what is important in life. That constitutes love, courage and bravery.

The symbolism of tying the rope around each other, so they stay together, as the cord of life, cooperation and connectedness speaks of phrases as: I'm here with you; we are in this together; we can make it as a team.

Pacing together back and forth from the front of the house to the back of the house as staying in rhythm with each other and the storm. Moving with the tide. Becoming one with the water current outside.

Returning to the ground floor with the water because of being *more curious than afraid.* Wanting to know what is going on.

When the sea comes in the house, it doesn't leave and stay out. It keeps returning, washing again and again, upping the ante for trusting the process.

What will this young man tell his child of his experience? How will he model the love, bravery and courage in his everyday life. How has he because of his experience changed his DNA and the DNA of his child?

How has Katrina changed all of our DNA?

"Getting Rid of Clutter"

The Reverend Doctor Jane Stanley was born in Gulfport, Mississippi and lived in Scotland for a year. She also lived in the French Quarter before returning to Gulfport to minister to a community called The Nourishing Place. An example of her ministry is during Katrina she housed 11 people to keep them out of harm's way. Some of these people were over 80. The following five people are some of those who stayed with Jane and her husband Max. Gail Cotton, Jane's partner-in-crime, was born in Detroit, Michigan and came to the Delta as a two year old. She also lived in the French Quarter and arrived in Gulfport in the late 80's. Carmen Engram came to the Coast in 1966 from the Philippines; she describes herself as "Navy People." She and her husband Bob stayed with Jane and Max. Heather White, Jane's daughter-in-law, came to the Coast in the Fall of 2001. She stayed at Jane's with her 4 year old daughter Camille and a ten day old baby.

Jane: I never entertained leaving this house.

Gail: This little house withstood Camille.

Carmen: I decided to leave at the last minute so I changed the sheets on the bed and came back to clean the house. At the last minute I wanted to be north of the railroad tracks. My daughters, crying and begging, called Jane to get me and Bob.

Heather: Sunday at 3:30 p.m. I was not that concerned and I had a ten day old baby and Camille who is 4 years old. I talked to Jane and felt it was better to be here with family. Jamie, my husband, called and said that the winds were 175 mph and we had waited too long to evacuate. Next time, I'll leave if it's a tropical depression. It was not scary, just a lot of rain and wind. After the hurricane there was a deafening quiet. The chain saws went all night, you heard men talking and dogs barking.

Jane: We were standing here and watching all the trees fall.

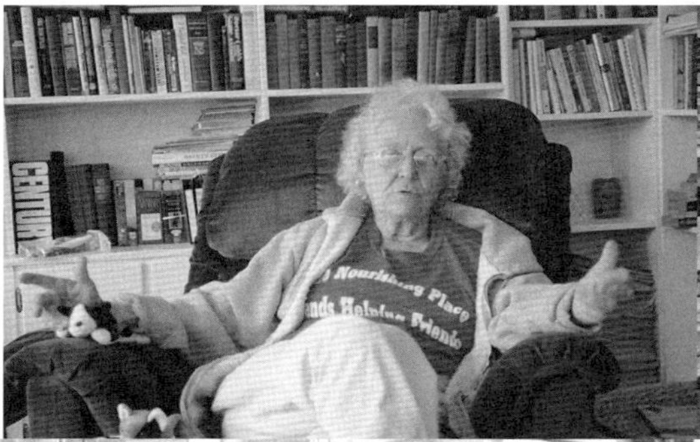
CENTURY

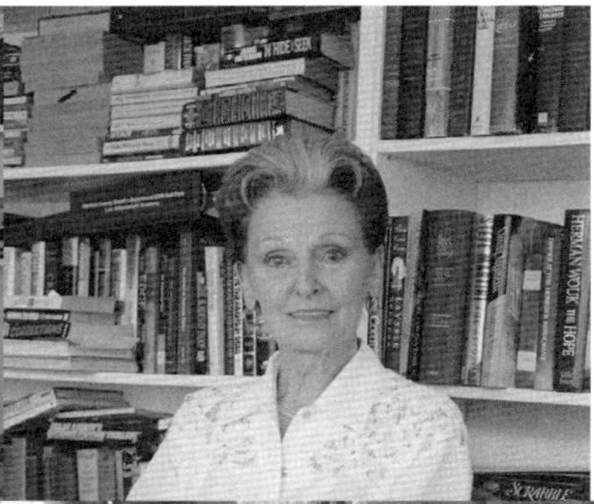
HERMAN WOUK
THE HOPE
SCRABBLE

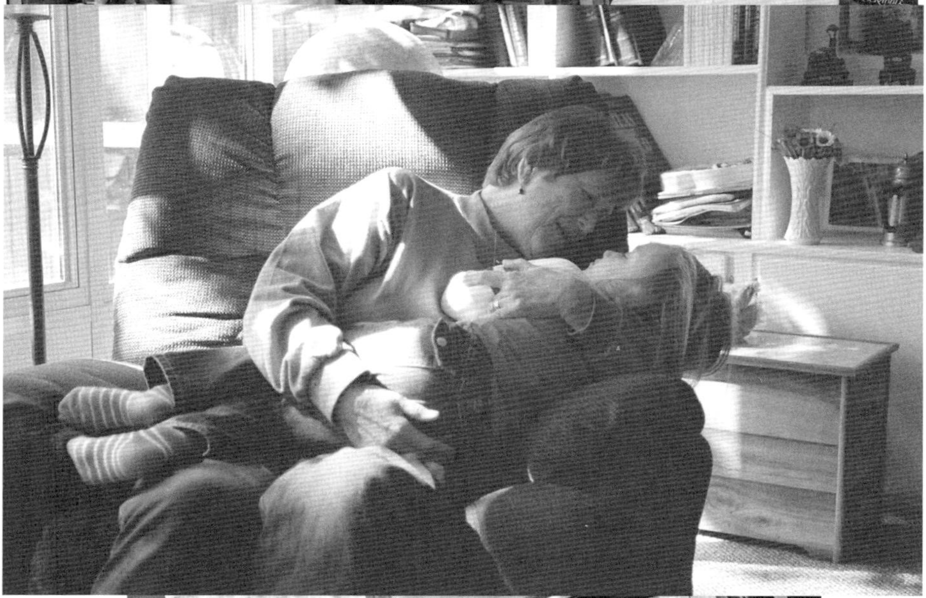

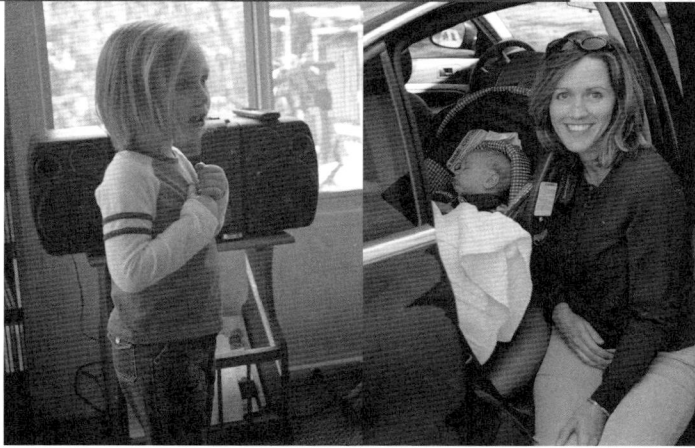

Carmen: I watched the pecan tree go very slowly.

Heather: I said, "I better move over the tree is falling," but none hit the house.

Jane: The aftermath was, how could it be that Carmen's house was washed away?

Jane & Heather: There was a constant wind. We talked about the tornadoes and where to go.

Jane: The wind was whistling through like a tunnel.

Carmen: There was a turtle who came in with the water. After a huge gust of wind we went into the bathroom and hallway to be safe from the tornadoes.

Jane: When the water came in, I was planning where to put everyone out of the water's reach.

Gail: We were praying the water would recede quickly.

Heather: The water was coming in from the back and then the front. I was so concerned that the water kept rising and rising from the creek. Then the wind pushed it out. The turtle stayed after the water went down.

Jane: We had a good time. We had coffee. Watched TV. It was like a camp with all ages.

Heather: It was good because there were so many people.

Jane: There were 11 people who stayed in all: Bob and Carmen; stepmother Rachel; Joan and Stehen Lindle; Gail; two babies and Heather; Max and Jane.

Camille: The four year old said the only time she was scared was when she didn't think that her dog could swim (the dog was moved to the shed).

Jane: We were feeding constantly.

Gail: The only reason I came was that Jane was adamant about coming.

Carmen: You want to stay in your own nest.

Jane: The electricity went off early about 4:00 a.m. I couldn't see to cook breakfast. But it seemed we were constantly eating.

Heather: I wondered when it would end! The TV said first 11:00 a.m., then 1:00 p.m. and then 3:00 p.m. I remember Ms. Carmen saying, "All I found was a butter knife from my silver."

Jane: What touched me so deeply was when Don told Carmen and Bob that everything was gone. Bob took Carmen in his arms and said, "We still have each other."

We were watching TV, WLOX, when we saw they had to leave the station because the roof was coming in and they showed the TV station.

Carmen: The bad part is afterwards. I lost everything, and then all of a sudden I was trying to get something to wear. I brought some rings, Bob's Georgia Tech ring. He said the only thing he wished he had was the Georgia Tech ring. I have my telephone book and address book. We went out at 7:00 p.m. and when I looked around and saw looters with a bag it made me so mad. If they were looking for food it would have been okay. A child had a bag on its arm.

Jane: Gail walked the primitive camp a long time.

Gail: Everything we built was still standing, there was no damage to any buildings in the primitive camp.

Jane: The next morning we went to Heather's and had to wind our way down the railroad track. "We were amazed because in front of the house was an arch from the Great Southern Golf Course. It was there, right in front. It was a solid 50 feet across. It had to have floated there. There was no water in her house. When Camille went into her room she said, "My room is broken--a tree came down."

Heather: One thing I learned is I will evacuate early; I am not a good traffic person. Stress was not from fear of the storm but the aftermath: the lack of coordination, the chaos afterwards, and the heat and no fresh water.

Carmen: When you finally realize that nothing is there; it is not your stuff or belongings that are as important as you thought they were. Values change. Things aren't as important. It's okay if fingernails break.

Jane: I was covered in a rash from head to toe after I put my feet in the creek behind my home to cool off. It was so hot. The night before I spilled a pot of boiling water on my knees and I went to the Chapel to get Gail and said, "I got to get to the hospital." We wound our way to Memorial. There were no lights. This rash even broke out on my hands and palms. A doctor from Jackson (young) saw me and said, "Do you have Syphilis?" I got another older doctor who thought it was some contact (with contamination) I was red as a shirt from head to toe. They gave me two shots.

Carmen: I went to Mobile and then Houston. I got chased out of Houston by Hurricane Rita. Then I went to Lafayette and rode out Rita in Lafayette. Now when you say misplaced (losing my home) this nest I've made (creating my home), the twigs are gone (the complete structure is gone).

Jane: My friends who had exquisite things from around the world lost everything and it really bothers me. For three Sundays straight I preached about getting rid of clutter.

Gail: We are calling it the "cleansing." I felt like the Lord knew I would never get around to cleaning up.

Carmen: When you have things, you don't think about it as much. But it is kind of nice to have a place of your own, a nest. I've been at many people's places. I guess I'm tired. I learned the value of friendship.

Jane: People are not able to find out and get answers about insurance, etc. People are frustrated.

Carmen: I wish I hadn't cleaned the house so much or polished the silver so often. The greatest thing I learned was, I realized, when I went back to the house and everything was turned upside down, it is the treasures you find. Everyone has been so wonderful.

Jane: Growing up here, I've been through lots of hurricanes. I like storms but have a little fear of trees coming falling on the house. So much has come out of this storm. The aftermath forced one to be more patient. The frustration is high. I feel badly for people who need answers. I guess every time there is a storm I remember the absolute power of nature. I also know I can't get along without friends. What was amazing to me is that for five days there was not a leaf showing, and then overnight there were leaves that popped out chartreuse.

Gail: Every time I walk into my house and see all the debris I think of the quote (Gail is almost 80):

> Living each day,
> For the very first time,
> Leaves us whole or tattered.
> In 80 years of things sublime,
> 'Twas the human touch
> That mattered.

I found a photo of my youngest daughter and my favorite hanging owl. All the treasures floated to the top and I salvaged them. These are things to put in my house when I get back.

Carmen: Someone brought me something the other day. The Chief of Naval Operations had written a most beautiful letter and someone found it. I was so glad, and it was wet. It is the only thing I had of 30 years in the Navy. It was written a long time ago.

Jane: I relearned that unhappiness is not caused by circumstances but by the condition of the mind--E. Tolle

Carmen: Abe Lincoln said, "You're going to be just about as happy as you make up your mind to be." I have no desire to buy a lot of things. I'm perfectly content. It is a strange feeling.

Musings

Bits and pieces of memories of our lives are scattered around or completely washed away. Coming back together is an individual process. When you lose everything you do not remember each individual object. At first I was not concerned with losing all my stuff. When asked what I felt was the greatest loss, I replied loss of community. It really is about the community of spirit.

What I was forgetting about the loss was not about all the things. It was about losing my home, the place I created that had held such wonderful memories. It was where I started my first meditation group. It was where I finished writing my doctoral thesis. It was a place where I and others did healing work. Friends would come and stay when I was gone during the summer to keep the energy flowing. It was where I would look out in the morning and see the water and sometimes the dolphins. I could take a few steps and be on the beach. I could take walks along the water to meditate or get in touch with my feelings. Those walks helped me relieve a depression I had in the late 1990s. Many people came to my home to visit. Some would just drop in unexpectedly and what a joy that was! I was right on Route 90. People would go by and honk their horn if they saw me on my porch or even if they did not see me there. The energy in my home and the friends that frequented it wrapped me in a cocoon of love, support, peace, caring, and kindness. And I had created this space. This is the real loss, not the things or structure.

When I remembered some of the things that I lost, I began to realize that the memory and energy attached to them was important to grieve. Getting in touch with my feelings helps me experience the grieving. Then I can let go.

I had lived in my condo on the the Gulf of Mexico in Pass Christian, Mississippi for nine out of the twelve years I have been on the Coast.

"Interesting Storm"

Garry McLain moved to the Coast on May 1, 2002, from West Richland, Washington where he had a horse ranch with his wife Linda. He also ran a small minimum security prison work-release program that was certified as a drug treatment center. Garry and Linda lived in Pass Christian on Henderson Point until building a new house and moving to Waveland February 2003. In 1975 Garry began having lung problems and had lung reduction surgery. In 1998 while in Seattle he began using oxygen for the first time. After moving to Waveland, Garry had a lung transplant in November of 2003. Then in February of 2005 he had what was probably a pulmonary embolism from the chronic rejection of the lung. In July 2005, he was in a hyperbaric chamber for forty treatments.

Katrina was the lowest pressure hurricane to hit the US. With low pressure you get shortness of breath, asthma develops and there is constriction of the air flow to the lungs. I felt the effects on Friday, August 26th. On Saturday I talked to Ochsner (hospital in New Orleans). Due to my shortness of breath they felt it was better to check into the hospital instead of being on the road in a traffic jam.

I checked into Hancock Medical Center, Saturday evening 8:30-9:00. Linda stayed Saturday at the hospital until I was stable and visited again Sunday morning. We then discussed what Linda was going to do. We decided it best for Linda to take the cat and take a few things and evacuate. She wanted to keep free of the traffic jam. When you go through the lung stuff that I have, you learn what to do and how to survive. I realize I'm terminally ill but I'm staying around.

Linda made it to my uncle's in Hattiesburg. I have to give a lot of credit to the hard working medical staff. They did the best they could with extremely limited resources for 33 patients. One example is late Sunday. The heavy rains caused the roof to leak into the third floor of the hospital where the staff was living. The staff moved to the second floor and moved the patients to the first floor except for intensive care. That worked okay until the storm came in with hurricane force winds.

Through my window, I could look out and see trees bending. Patients across the hall saw trees fall down and hit cars. There were buckets of water coming down and very strong winds.

About 10:00 a. m. Monday, everyone started to panic because everyone had to go to the second floor due to the storm surge. I'm in a wheelchair on the first floor and the water is nine inches deep on the floor. It came up rather rapidly. The elevator was not working. We did not have electricity, food, or water. The sewers began to back up on the first floor. As I am being pushed down the hall as fast as they can, we go past the glass door and see three feet of water outside.

We go up the stairs which was the only option with me trying to walk. Someone is pushing behind me. I am pulling on the railing as much as I could and grasping air for each breath I take while the eye wall of the hurricane is passing over the hospital at the same time. I managed to get up the stairs. The entire first floor was wiped out. The wind had broken out the glass in the waiting room and water had poured in at that point. The kitchen, radiology, medical records lab, and emergency room, the entire first floor were all wiped out.

At the time the phones went out, Linda and I lost contact and the hurricane was coming through Hattiesburg as a Category 1. Linda worried about what was going on and I worried about her.

On Monday (August 29th) evening there were generators for the hospital that were wiped out during that day. We had no power whatsoever. We used little glow lights that were hung from the sprinkler system so we could see. We had no running water and no food services. We had some water in liter bottles. We had one liter a day and the food staff had peanut butter and jelly. Our bulk food came from snack machine, Fritos, 3 Musketeers, Snickers, and peanuts became survival food. Occasionally we got lights running and AC. It is hot as hell in August. We had fans blowing on us and we went outside.

Tuesday after the storm everyone was in a state of shock at the hospital and surrounding community. At 1:30 in the afternoon the Florida medical investigators had a satellite phone and two helicopters. The intensive care patients and two pregnant ladies got to Mobile, Alabama in time for delivery. One of them was not sure about riding in a helicopter. She was pretty much in a state of panic.

On the second helicopter I was supposed to go, but a guy was riding a motorcycle and broke his pelvis and had other trauma so he was taken to a major trauma center. Six were taken out on Tuesday with new patients coming in that were heavily injured.

We stayed the next night, Tuesday. The oxygen continued to work the whole time. It ran off liquid oxygen in a real big tank.

Lo and behold, three ambulances from Memphis came down Tuesday night. They were told to come to Hancock County and told to park in the parking lot. They got no further instructions. The doctor commandeered the ambulances.

The Red Cross found us Wednesday at 11:00 and gave us MRE's, Sweet and Sour Chicken. It tasted so good. At 11:35 my lung partner and I went into an ambulance with two guys that needed dialysis. We went to Jackson, to the University Medical Center with the four of us in one ambulance and the other two ambulances which had two and three red lights and sirens all the way. As I was leaving the medical center I saw people still trying to evacuate. The devastation was beyond belief.

When I went through triage in the Medical Center, they brought in only the injured Hurricane Katrina people. A nurse contacted Linda through her cell phone. It was Wednesday evening around supper time about 6:00 p.m. and the nurse told Linda that they would have me situated in a room and that Linda could call in an hour. The nurses are the backbone of the medical system and were very sensitive to the needs of families to make contact. I was very appreciative of them.

In Hattiesburg the hurricane was a Category 1 and still they had no power, telephones, or water. They had a lot of damage. My uncle, aunt and cat were fine. My aunt was 89 at the time and my Uncle is 86. Linda and my uncle were able to get their yard cleaned and this helped keep her busy.

Unfortunately, during that period of time I lost 15 pounds (some water and some muscle). I had a limited amount of mobility in the hospital with a 25 foot oxygen tether. So my muscles atrophied quite a bit.

When I got home from the University Hospital in Jackson on September 9th, I could not walk more than 25 steps before having to rest or sit down. By mid-October I was able to enter a physical rehabilitation program by doing what I could to get stronger. I rested a lot and took a few steps more each day.

Due to the monitored exercises, by Thanksgiving I was able to walk a third of a mile and drive the Toyota truck my son gave me to replace the one I lost in the hurricane. I felt like a human being again because I had some freedom to drive myself wherever I wanted to go.

It's taken me quite a bit to get my muscles back. I'm still not there. I've had two setbacks. One time at Ochsner's Hospital. I still have a I.V. port in my arm.

While in the hospital at Ochsner's there was miscommunication of medications I was given too much Coumadin. I got a double dose five days then they brought it down. Monday this week, January 30, 2006, the blood vessel in my right eye burst. From 10:30 Monday night until 4:00 a.m. we were in the emergency clinic at Forest General. The opthomologist stated that there would be no permanent damage to the eye but it would take six weeks to two months to heal. My wife said it looked like I was shot with a shotgun. I am getting physical therapy which is slowly building my muscles back.

During the storm there were moments I panicked, but overall I was okay. I felt support from the staff at the medical center. They made sure we were going to survive and do well given the resources they had. The dash through the water and upstairs was scary as hell and physically demanding. Not being able to reach Linda was frightening.

The care was good. The director of nursing was helpful. The idea to break into the snack machine and the insistence of the doctor to have an evacuation plan was important for our survival. These decisions helped reduce the panic even though it took the Red Cross so long to find out we existed.

There is overall resentment and frustration and anger with the emergency management because it seems like the folks in Hancock County got short-shifted. They received less attention from the news media, etc. This includes FEMA, MEMA and it still irks me.

The housing after the storm has been an ongoing saga. They offered us eight different trailers at our property which has no sewer, water or electricity. I'm on oxygen and can't go into a gas-fired trailer. Finally my neighbor said put one in even though there was no way to connect it. Eventually we said we needed a special needs trailer. We were going to hook it up at St. Rose de Lima (church) but there was no sewer hook up.

One practitioner was going to let us put a mobile home on her property and tried to install it but the street was too narrow. Then the doctor from Ochsner said the dust and dirt and mold was too much on the Coast for me.

So I was going to get a trailer on a lot I found and then Fema changed the rules. They gave me a travel trailer 12' x 40' with a 12' x 12' ADA bathroom, which is wheelchair accessible in the shower, and a ramp I did not need. There was no closet space.

It was like a Frankenstein thing, so we turned that down and began looking for an apartment. We moved in December 23 to a nice two bedroom duplex. So I'm at rest now until we can move back to the Coast. We love the Coast.

We've evacuated from Washington State because of wildfires and from St. Helen's in the 80's. Why would hurricanes be any different? The midwest has tornadoes. The west coast has earthquakes and there are wildfires in Washington State. Pick your poison. I happen to love the Coast. We'll be back.

I don't know if I changed that much or learned a lot from Katrina given my circumstance with my lung condition and the rapid form of rejection. Over the last 30 plus years I've been dealing with death, Death threats in the corrections job and with the illness, you recognize you are going to die.

My father and grandfather were funeral directors. The fear of death and idea of dying is not new to me. I realize I have a terminal illness. Katrina is just another chapter in that.

I still firmly find myself on some level of spiritual commitment and alone. I know there is a greater power. I may not be conscious of it. Death is not the end of everything. So it doesn't frighten me that much.

It could be called reincarnation. The Big Mystery doesn't have an end. Just another step in life. I had such spiritual conversations with Father Sebastian at the St. Rose church.

I am really missing my church. There are 29 different churches around the country that adopted St. Rose as a parish to support. The outpouring of love and support from outside has been incredible. The individuals with FEMA etc., have tried so hard. They are good folks trying hard in a disastrous situation.

"Interesting storm" is an interesting term. It reminds me of my high school days when the girls at the proms had fancy hairdos and asked you what you thought. Interesting doesn't really describe anything or explain anything. You could use interesting as a neutral word.

I want to get back home. No way to get back home. The house we built to spend the rest of our life in is all wiped out, neighbors, flowers, etc. never to be replicated.

We are no different from the 100,000 others. Nothing significant except personal loss. You can't focus on that.

Musings

Nothing dies; it only changes form.

I think there's a way of training ourselves in order not to become the victim of fear and grief--that is to look deeply into ourselves and see that we are made of non-self elements, like a father looking at his children can see his continuation in his children. So he is not attached to the idea that his body is the only thing that is him. He's more than his body. He is inside of this body but he is also at the same [time] outside of his body in many elements. And if we have the habit of looking like that, we will not be the victim of our attachment to one form of manifestation, and we will be free. And that freedom makes happiness and peace possible.

Long Live Impermanence, Interview with Thich Nhat Hanh by Lisa Schneider *Sacred Pathways*, April/May 2004 Vol. 7 No 2, page 25

"Lord, Look at my House"

Mary Reynolds grew up in the Delta and came to the Coast in 1966. She has been catering for 16-18 years and now also has the Gumbo House in Gulfport, which is frequented by many locals who enjoy real Southern cooking.

I was trying to get my house boarded up and by the time that I did, the traffic was blocked up so I couldn't get out. I went to my ex-husband's in Gulfport close to Interstate 10. My house is right on the tracks. I thought I'd be safer up there.

I was nervous and afraid because the house was shaking, the trees were falling and we got lots of wind. The French doors were rattling, and he was constantly trying to keep those doors closed. All my children and most of my grandchildren were at the house with us.

I came back right after the storm, 2:30-3:00 p.m. to see my house. The lines were down and the trees were down. I had to come around Sav-a-Center to come back after the storm.

The inside of my house fell out. Shoes and pictures were all outside. The shingles and tar paper were off; I had roof damage and the ceiling fell down in the house. Trees were down in the yard. My front door and porch was tilted.

I said, "Lord, look at my house." I never cried! I just said, "I know it's going to be okay!"

I know I changed a lot. I don't put that much importance on things anymore. I know the storm brought us closer to God. The time since the storm not having food, ice, electricity has taught me that. I stayed in my house; I had no other place to live. We got it cleaned out. Until last week I stayed in it. Now the church is fixing it up.

My daughter lost everything, her apartment with one bedroom, a den and kitchen.

I am a strong believer in gas. I can take a match and light that stove. I'm country so I know how to flip bread on top of the stove. My neighbor had electric so we had breakfast at my house and grilled at his house for dinner. We set up a kitchen in his garage.

My whole neighborhood came together. It was just like family. I'm the mommy on the street. We all get together. They come and see how I am. We're like one big happy family.

Musings

Our ancestors cooked around a fire and now we cook around a barbecue grill. Katrina has brought us together as we gather around grills and stoves to share our meals and our stories. We all have a story and it seems everyone is eager to listen and share. Storytelling is having a new revival. We are getting back into the ancient art of the Bards.

Bonfires on the beach are a big thing here. Not only on holidays would you see many people gathered there around a fire, enjoying the flames and having food with friends and family. The day of firewood stacked and piled like a teepee let you know it was happening. At dusk the fire would be lit. People gathered, talked, ate and told stories.

On June 21, 2005, the first day of summer, bonfires were planned to celebrate life and peace, one at each of the seven towns along the Coast. They were in Ocean Springs, Biloxi, Gulfport, Long Beach, Pass Christian, Bay St. Louis, and Waveland. We had 300 + people, young and old. Biloxi had the Buddhist monks whom we chanted with and then we sang our peace song together. There was drumming at Ocean Springs, Biloxi, Long Beach, and Pass Christian also had some Belly Dancing. In Long Beach and other sites prayers for peace were recited in 12 different religious traditions. We came together in all our diversity forming a circle around a fire. We ate and built community. Some people had never been on the beach before for a bonfire.

Stories now seem to be on deeper levels, relating the human condition of late. With this exchange we have become more open to each other, having come through this storm together. We are going through the process of opening our hearts, more and more and need to keep opening even when we think we have gone as far as we can.

The stories that seem to be enjoyed most are the faux pas with FEMA. These receive the biggest and best belly laughs. In its own way, FEMA, with its lack of coordination and efficiency, is helping to relieve our stress so we can heal. Humor is one of the best ways to release our pent up frustrations. Laugh well, laugh long and hard!

"Everyone is Different"

David Reynolds and Robert Wedekind moved to the Coast on December 31, 1999 and celebrated the millennium here.

David: We didn't leave because I decided after Ivan I would rather die than go 13 miles an hour for 13 hours, in grid lock. In order to get me to evacuate I'd need to be out of grid lock, out of food (has a special diet), gas, etc. We had rice, food, generator and all these things to support us. I had made up my mind I wasn't going. We didn't even watch the news, see TV or know the eye was coming here.

Robert: The talking heads on TV hype a very negative aspect they dream up and sell as hype. "What if, what if, after two days of this you die in no shape to do anything. Our friend Holly said the psychological impact of the media from the hype is detrimental. I listened to the weather radio and checked in every hour.

David: Robert has an expensive bed, and we had a little bit of water, two to three inches. It was scary as it came through the door. We raised the bed on an eight inch block as soon as we got the water. The water started going out so we put the bed on rollers so we could move it to get up the carpet. The dog was calm and I was calm telling Robert what to do.

Robert: We've been meditating for five years religiously every single day. Had we not had that experience we would have have experienced the storm differently. We both dropped into a lower state of calmness, a meditative state, an abnormal state, an opposite state to the storm. There was nothing normal about this calmness. As the storm escalated we got calmer, below the normal, in a relaxed state. There was some kind of grace that came to us. It was something outside ourselves. It is a grace that comes from a collective consciousness that comes down upon you. I've been around a lot of AIDS patients who experience this right before death. A grace in dying and they (AIDS patients) become the caregivers.

We did some bailing of water and all that. I was getting tired and I said, "Mother Mary I'm getting a little tired, how much longer do we have to do this?" I heard her voice say, "In 45 minutes it will be over." I walked out in the street to the minute and it was over. It was the female presence. I didn't make the 45 minutes up. It took the edge off.

David: We had a lot of time. We moved things and looked from the deck upstairs. We saw the water was up three feet on the washer and dryer. During the flooding we were very, very busy. The wind was way before the flood. The wind started about 5:30-6:30 a.m. and the electricity went off. The gas was okay until about 12:00. I went for a walk with the dog at 4:30 a.m. I was not prepared for anyone that was crazy.

There was a pine tree you could see outside the window which let us know how hard it was blowing.

The generator was a nightmare. Robert took the carburetor apart in the back yard.

Robert: There is a theory about karmically-induced negative consciousness. Some people say that's what the storm was about, and we were in the center of it. I believe if you can be in the center of this negative consciousness and ask for grace, it will come to you in the midst of it all. You can be of any faith.

And after that we had three to four weeks of survival mode.

David: The only time from August 29 through September that I was scared was when we were told by the police that if we left the check point at Espy and 2nd, we couldn't come back. Martial law. It was scary. We were planning on going someplace but had a dog at home, so we turned around and came back. We stayed a couple of hours then went to the fire station. We had no water to drink and had some food. At my age, I'm not scared of anything.

Robert: The martial law reminds me of the search and seizure laws which are taking away our freedom. On another level because of our growth, the old system is dying and we are experiencing a tremendous rebirth. It is overwhelming.

David: Both of us have said to each other that if we had lost everything, it wouldn't matter. We didn't lose any stuff and were okay. Right after the storm we started cutting trees and fixing the fence.

Robert: I wanted to find normalcy as soon as possible. I wanted to make the house look normal so other people would start feeling a sense of home. The dog was crazy for three days and he was approaching people who weren't there. He was in a daze walking down the middle of the street. I was in front trying to get his attention and he was oblivious to me. It was like "nobody is home." "Bugs" was sniffing at people, walking up to them and growling at inappropriate times.

Every place in the house had an essence. I know it was human because Bugs would sniff the feet then go up and down the body like he did with humans before. He never did it before or since. It was normal behavior for abnormal times.

David: What I learned from the storm was I don't need to leave, maybe go to a shelter but how safe is that? We have a six million dollar estate in front of us. During Camille it did not have any water. On Wisteria the water came to the same place as in Camille. The man who lives three houses off the beach, he broke his finger before Katrina. He bought his house 20 years ago. His house didn't have any water during Camille and showed us where the line was, it was the same during Katrina.

Robert: The more we travel, we keep looking for answers. The more you study something of this magnitude, you come head to head with its unknowingness. It is unknowable. The consciousness is unknowable. It is beyond the human scope. It teaches you exactly what you are ready to be taught. Everyone is different. My grieving for other losses seems wondrous and yet we are both grieving about the same thing. How can you grieve when you lost everything; how can you grieve when you have everything? It is every bit as real for me to feel the grief of others and loss of others. It is the common denominator.

David: Every single leaf on every single tree is gone.

Robert: It is like the winter up north. For two to three weeks I never felt such a sense of cleanliness. It was a wondrous clean feeling. It went beyond consciousness.

David: It irritated both of us when people came back after three weeks and thought things would be okay. God put us here to take care of something. No one is taking care of something if they are sitting three weeks in a hotel and not taking care of their property.

Robert: I was the last person to talk to Holly before the storm. She said she would ride it out and we said we would, and we all have.

Musings

"When we become spiritualized by self-discipline and deep meditation, we soar like the wind in the omnipresence of our true soul-nature."

"The cultivation of intuitive calmness requires unfoldment of the inner life. When developed sufficiently, intuition brings immediate comprehension of truth. You can have this marvelous realization. Meditation is the way."

--Paramahansa Yogananda

"I Feel Blessed"

Melba Venison came to New Orleans in 1971 from Opelousas, Louisiana. She has lived in Lakeview for 28 years. Melba worked with grades K-12 in the public schools for 30 years. When she retired, she and her best friend Katie were asked to come work at SUNO (Southern University at New Orleans) to help with accreditation. After they arrived, the dean that hired them was fired and the next dean died. Then they met Rose Duhon Sells, who became the new Dean. She interviewed both Melba and Katie and they were hired. They initially intended to work for a year and it is now four years later and accreditation is coming back and they are still there.

I always leave for hurricanes. Katie and I, being friends for a long time, always called each other about storms. About three years ago we waited too long and got caught in traffic for five hours in Baton Rouge. I promised if the Lord gets us out of this mess I'll never let this happen again.

Since that time whenever hurricane season approaches I laugh and say, "These people can stay if they want; we are leaving." We didn't want to be caught in traffic again so we would leave three-four days before the storm.

We were at SUNO and they were hesitant about closing early. We got our stuff and left early. This time was no different. Katie and I laugh about it that we'd be gone way before everyone and they would be stuck in traffic. It was the traffic that would make us leave.

During Katrina, I left Saturday morning before the hurricane because I had elderly parents. I had to go and secure my parents in Lafayette. They are in their nineties and I had to get them out so we wouldn't get caught in traffic.

I went to Baton Rouge that day. I felt it was okay once we were out of New Orleans. There is only one way out of NOLA. When the hurricane changed direction, we went to Lake Charles to my brother's to wait out the hurricane there.

Lo and behold, we all thought we'd only be gone a couple of days. I had only a couple of clothes with me. I was in Lake Charles and watched TV and I was floored. I said, "That's my house! That's my neighborhood!" All the images on TV and all the ones I saw, I never thought my house would flood.

I had a huge oak, 150 years old, anchored in my backyard in the corner. The oak tree hung over my house. I liked it because it gave a lot of shade. My house is not scorching hot because of the tree. My husband and I would always laugh that the oak tree would fall and crush this house. My son had his room by the tree and he always said his room was cooler than the rest of the house. We'd always laugh that "one big wind and the tree would fall on the house." Every year I said I'd get the tree limbs cut. They were really big.

During the hurricane, I kept thinking that the tree fell on my house. When I finally got back, the tree had fallen. Lightning split the tree in half. One side fell on one neighbor's yard and the other side on the other neighbor's yard. I had only leaves on my roof. The first thing I saw was the tree and I said, "The one time I need that tree to fall on my house for the insurance and it falls on my neighbor's."

The second thing that happened was when we went around and walked into my house, I thought I must be in another country, another cosmos, it was awful. It looked smaller. It was closed and dark and shallow and dreary and it didn't look like my house. Everything was brown and turned over. Three weeks to a month had passed before I had come back.

On the dinette set I had a vase with a plant and water in it with ivy. The plant was twelve feet, gorgeous, blue green in the middle of the wooden table. I had twelve feet of water in my house. Everything had probably flooded as the water came in and the plant went up with the water and came down on the table. The table was broken and yet the plant had water in it. It was BEAUTIFUL! It had grown twelve inch branches. The leaves were so huge it looked like a philodendron, not an ivy. Everything else was broken and and all the other plants were dead.

My sister said, "Take the plant." I felt it was demonic so I left it. We left and I came back two weeks later and the plant had grown another one to two inches. The original water had evaporated from full to about one quarter. I didn't water it. The plant was absolutely gorgeous. I took it and put it outside and said, "You don't belong in here. I don't know if you are a good or bad boy." With all the destruction, the death and stillness of life in that house and that plant survived. My den was nothing but plants and I had ficas, shifilaras, etc. I said I needed to pull in the ozone layer from these plants.

Everything was dead but that ivy plant was okay. That water in the plant was not dirty, it was clear. It had to have floated. It was incredible, absolutely incredible.

I think of all the people who have been affected very negatively, and I am amazed at myself by my calmness and my ability to deal with all the issues that surround that hurricane.

I have no house. I feel like a nomad. My son has no house to come home to and yet I feel hopeful, I feel blessed because there are so many people who have extended themselves to me. People whose lives before you only touched slightly.

I am grateful that I have a job. I think the one thing that stands out for me is I have such a strong circle of friends and family. I can't say enough about my sister and her husband who live in Baton Rouge. I live with them. They have a big house and I have my own place there. We share the kitchen. My brother-in-law is always bringing things. We grew up close. I expected this of family. I've noticed my son is strong, he is like a rock for me.

We had 30 teachers in the department at SUNO and after Katrina we are down to six. I can't say enough about the people I work for.

It was so good when we, SUNO, went to Baton Rouge to teach. We were forced to go to Baton Rouge and we were in one room together. I first thought we'll all be on each other. I think because we were all in the same boat we bonded. We laughed together, we cried together. I went there in the morning to see what we would laugh about.

We had war stories about our houses, war stories about insurance. When we were told we had to come to New Orleans we thought we would commute so we could get back to the cleaner air in Baton Rouge. Traffic was so bad during the commute that I'm staying in Rose's house in New Orleans during the week.

I work with a wonderful group of people. I love them all. We work so well together. I'm so proud of Rose, she will turn this school around. Rose is now Vice President for Academic Affairs at SUNO.

My work has saved my life. My friends have saved my life. I try to be very spiritual. I've made peace with all of that because I know who's in charge. It's been okay.

I lost a baby when I was married about ten years. That was very difficult for my husband and I. But I came to understand the Lord is in charge and I don't need to understand. We are all on borrowed time. I'm just preparing my son for when I'm not here.

Since the hurricane it hasn't been the destruction that is a problem (as if the loss of community wasn't enough). It is much bigger than that.

I ran into my neighbor whose son was clearing out her house and he said, "I can't believe this, everything I knew is gone. My community is gone. Ms. Melba, you held my hand when I needed it. I don't even have my year book. Your son Marcus and I played ball out here." I said, "It will come back." He said, "It is my neighborhood, my history that is gone. A piece of me no longer exists. This house, when it's rebuilt, won't have that same feel or energy."

In New Orleans to grow up and help your children survive in a black neighborhood is special. We all raised the kids on my block. Particularly to raise African-American males you better have lots of support and people to help you. My neighbor on the left is a principal; my neighbor across the street is a doctor. We've been there 30 years. One of my neighbors retired. Prior to that time we had a neighbor with a daughter, now in Vanderbilt, who didn't have a father. She'd come to sit on my husband's lap when she wanted to feel safe.

FEMA, etc. is after the fact. It is not as important as my neighborhood. It was not high class. It was important to me because they were good people.

Musings

How do we replace a neighborhood? Can we do that? Maybe the best we can do is start anew and use our learnings from the past to pave the future. Can we be present and work from where we are? In the present moment it is possible to find guidance. This is the place of spirit that guided this story teller to go back to teaching and find the miracle of a growing plant among devastation and destruction. Curious, isn't it?

Maybe the neighborhood becomes where you work. The energy of a strong bonding in a community will not leave anyone who lived there. It will be carried in each and every one of their spirits wherever they go. It will spread far and wide to places never thought possible before Katrina.

The spirit in this neighborhood and many other neighborhoods similar to it with strong bonding and love will go out to many states in these United States. The energy of these spirited souls will go out and ignite and change the hearts, minds and souls of this country. That strength, commitment and connection is not isolated to a place. This is about the people and what flows in their hearts.

Epilogue

Katrina waltzes into people's homes, does a little two step and goes out again. She repeats this process over and over again for ten hours. As we can see, the waltz is not always the same. Sometimes there's a dip or a dive. Sometimes she sweeps you off your feet. One major thing she has done for many is to help people open up their hearts, over and over again. She has people of different cultures coming together in community as a tapestry of many colors. We get a taste of our oneness, our sameness, our connection. Do we continue this waltz?

The following updates tell how our storytellers are still waltzing. Rochelle Roberson has moved to Charlotte, North Carolina. She now manages a Blockbuster store there. There are some adjustments. She went from living alone for five years to having a roommate. She is making new friends and even though she wanted to leave the Coast, she misses it at times.

Arman Codianne is considering rebuilding his home. He has applied for a grant. He has received a minor settlement from his insurance company. If he gets his full insurance coverage, he will be able to pay off his mortgage.

Lee Emery is working and living it day to day. She has worked on the duplex to fix it up to rent. When she sees something that reminds her of the past she says, "Oh my!" She isn't dwelling on the past.

Cathy Brugger and her husband John have been approved for a SBA personal property loss loan. It looks like they will build a home in Mobile where John works. While building they might live in a FEMA trailer on Cathy's mother's property.

Gwendolyn Canon is growing weary. She realizes it will take a long time to rebuild the Pass. She did get her carpet for her upstairs bedroom. Teaching school has helped her recover. Volunteers have come to the school and have been a great help for her and the children.

She took a break this Spring to visit her mother. She begins to worry about getting ready for hurricane season and where she will put all her stuff since her shed was destroyed. Driving along the water on the now opened Route 90 every day to go to work has been fun for her and seems to bring her peace.

John McManus had surgery since the storm and is recovering well. On March 3rd he got a home in Saucier inside the Desoto National Forest. He says, "It is really beautiful and we're really happy here." Once in a while, he has weird dreams and an attack of melancoly.

Brian Murphy has a new job selling portable buildings and spas and a new truck. He was not able to buy the home he was renting. He has moved to Edgewater Park in Biloxi next to the Mall.

Garry McLain was sent home from the hospital in Hattisberg because they could no longer do anything for him. Father Sabastian from St. Rose's parish visited him. On April 20, his wife Linda called me and said Garry was off all of his medication. He was fading in and out of consciousness. We are all praying for a peaceful transition for him and for peace for Linda. Garry passed away on May 5 at 2:00 a.m. There was a service on the beach in Waveland.

Mary Reynolds is still rebuilding her home.

Jayson Sutkus and Leslie Wilder are experiencing tremendous peace coming to them. Leslie said, "We are placing our hearts in our home and working from the inside out." They are busy rebuilding their Reiki house.

Coastal residents are not the only ones waltzing. Thousands of college students did a reversed two step and waltzed down to the Mississippi Coast and New Orleans to help with the cleanup after Katrina instead of partying during their spring break. They said they will be back this summer to continue to help.

Kent State students removed debris from my friend's property where I am putting my FEMA trailer. My friends were in Maine at the time. As these students were cleaning up the property they called me and told me they found a gold bracelet and wanted to know where to put it. I gave them a place and I picked it up the next day. I found it in a jar along with a ring and a Rune Stone (alphabet symbols used by our European ancestors to read into the future of things). My friends and I were very curious to find out what this one Rune meant since it was the only one left out of a set of 24. I consulted two books.

In *Runes in 10 Minutes* by R.T. Kaser, the Rune, which is shaped like an "H" stands for hail. This is what it said:

> The H Rune is about the powers of nature...to shape and mold the world...to change the environment...and help or hinder your safe passage. A storm must be kicking up in your neck of the woods. And I'd have to say all hail's about to break loose. Why else would a dark cloud be hovering over your head? Perhaps you'd best come in, before you catch a cold. The best you can do sometimes is weather these things. You need to ride out this storm. Batten down the hatches for now. Put tape on the windows. Make popcorn, and get out the hurricane lamps; Tomorrow is soon enough to pick up the pieces. *Traditional names: Hagalaz, The Hail, The Hailstone, White Stone of the Frost Giant, The Hail Egg.*

In *The Book of Runes* by Ralph H. Blum the H Rune further describes the coming events of Katrina.

> H stands for *Hagalaz* which means Disruption, Elemental Power and Hail. Change, freedom, invention and liberation are all attributes of this Rune. Drawing it indicates a pressing need within the psyche to break free from constricting identification with material reality and to experience the world of archetypal mind.

The Rune of elemental disruption, of events that seem to be totally beyond your control, *Hagalaz* has only an upright position, and yet it always operates through reversal. When you draw this Rune, expect disruption, for it is the Great Awakener, although the form the awakening takes may vary. Perhaps you will experience a gradual feeling of coming to your senses, as though you are emerging from a deep sleep. Then again, the onset of power may be such as to rip away the fabric of what you previously knew as your reality, your security, your understanding of yourself, your work, your relationships or beliefs.

Disruption takes many forms: a relationship fails, plans go awry, a source of supply dries up. But do not be dismayed. Whether you created the disruption, or whether it comes from an outside source, you are not without power in this situation. Your inner strength--the will you have funded until now in your life--provides support and guidance at a time when everything you've taken for granted is being challenged.

Another of the Cycle Runes, the term *radical discontinuity* best *describes* the action of *Hagalaz* at its most forceful. The more severe the disruption in your life, the more significant and timely the requirements for your growth. The universe and your own soul are demanding that you do, indeed, grow.

This is another example of our connectedness, our oneness. This Rune Stone from my friends' property is attuned with what my friends went through in having their home and all their possessions swept away. Katrina has been a major disruption for anyone who lives on the Gulf Coast or New Orleans. She has helped us all find our inner strength. And most of all she teaches us how we are all connected to each other and part of the oneness of God. She opened our hearts.

Many people have waltzed with Katrina: relief workers, Coast and New Orleans residents, Hispanic immigrants helping us rebuild, so many churches, towns from across the United States, countries like Saudi Arabia sending kitchens in a box, Vietnam offering money cards, FEMA workers who put in 12 hour days, the Salvation Army, the Red Cross, the list goes on and on. We could not have made the progress we have without them. They heard the call to dance. They remembered the connection. They waltzed. I continue to ask am I ready to continue to waltz with Katrina or for that matter with any disruption that occurs in my life? Will I remember the connection in every moment that God is with me and in all persons and all things around me? In every situation I can be at peace (see the connection) or be at war (see separation). I can waltz in every moment. I remember going to Mystery School and studying with Jean Houston; she said, "There is only the dance." Now I know what she meant. I choose waltzing!